MEDIA MANUALS

**Script Continuity
and the Production Secretary**

MEDIA MANUALS

Script Continuity
and the
Production Secretary
in Film and TV

Avril
Rowlands

FOCAL PRESS
London & Boston

Focal Press
is an imprint of the Butterworth Group
which has principal offices in
London, Boston, Durban, Singapore, Sydney, Toronto, Wellington

First published 1977
  Reprinted 1978, 1981, 1983, 1985

© Focal Press Limited, 1977

ISBN 0 240 50949 8

Printed and bound in Great Britain by A. Wheaton & Co. Ltd, Exeter

Contents

The Complete Continuity Girl

There you stand, dressed in your oldest jeans and thickest sweater (unless you're unbelievably lucky and start in fine weather): a stopwatch resting imposingly upon your bosom—maybe a Polaroid camera also—and a clipboard clutched as a lifeline in front of you. Pencils, ready sharpened, are secreted somewhere about your person; virginal continuity notes and unmarked pages of script lie neatly gathered under the large clip on top of your clipboard, and securely tethered (in case of high winds) with a large rubber band. You have left your typewriter perched on a couple of packing cases in the cowshed nearby. You may, being prepared for any eventualities, have a sheet of plastic covering the paperwork. In your capacious waterproof bag somewhere near your feet are spare copies of the script and the schedule, together with spare pens, pencils, adhesive tape, scissors—spares of everything, in fact, even down to the odd aspirin and safety pin. There you stand, ready for the off, a complete.... continuity girl.

Around you are the rest of the film unit, all equally uncomfortable despite the 'getting it together' drinks at the director's expense the previous evening. Everyone is bursting with the effort of being alert and appearing as impressive, busy and efficient as the others. One of the electricians cracks the first joke; the clapperboy comes up to you—or you go up to him—and he pledges to keep you informed of changes of camera roll. You, in turn, promise to keep an eagle eye on the slate numbers, and if he chalks up the wrong number, not to hold him up to general ridicule—at least, not in the first week of shooting. He says, not trying to be original, "How about starting with Slate 1?" and you duly laugh and agree.

The cameraman, alternately gazing with a worried frown at the sky and then staring at his exposure meter and shaking it with incredulity, stops to ask the director: "What's the first set-up?" The director interrupts his agitated first assistant, who is engaged in an earnest explanation of the lack of coffee/rolls/sausages and rushes over to his cameraman (who must be humoured). The first assistant has a go at the second assistant about the lack of coffee/rolls/sausages and the second assistant sends the third assistant off on a search. You become unwittingly involved with the boom operator who, under the guise of telling you the sound roll number—which, believe it or not, is roll one starts to get too familiar. This does nothing for your image on the first day of filming, so you leap off to the director and look concerned and interested while he explains his first shot to the camera crew.

Artistes have now been called for, and appear in a flurry of make-up assistants with large powder puffs and dressers with large safety pins. The director and first assistant are smothered in a round of complaints and embracings and the air is full of expressions in vogue with top artistes. The rest of the unit stand round looking rather bored, except for the electrician who is looking round for likely talent.

Rehearsals commence, and you write down everything from the colour of the grass to the markings on the third rock on the left of frame. As rehearsals continue you neatly rub out what you first wrote as moves are changed, and then you rub out the second lot of notes as things change again.

Finally, all is ready for a take. The first assistant calls for quiet, the director calls 'turn over', the sound recordist calls 'speed', the camera operator 'mark it', and the clapperboy, who's been itching to do his bit with the clapperboard for the last minute, claps it and jumps out of the way. You, having already written the scene, the slate, the description of the shot, the set-up and the artistes, are poised, one hand on the stopwatch, the other holding a razor sharp pencil.

The director calls 'action' and you're away. He almost instantly calls 'cut' due to heavy artillery fire from the army practice range two miles off. (The army wouldn't play ball and stop their activities for the filming.) The director casts a pained glance at the first assistant (who couldn't persuade the army); the first assistant casts a pained glance at the second assistant who hurries up to the third assistant (who has just arrived hotfoot and panting with the coffee etc.). The clapperboy painstakingly rubs out '1' and writes '2' on his board, with a stick of chalk embedded in a small piece of foam, attached to the clapperboard by a long clean piece of string. By the end of the shooting, the string is so well worn it has snapped off, and the 'hunt the chalk' game takes place hourly.

You write 'NG, noise' on your notes—the board is clapped, the army silenced, the gaffer electrician stops work in protest as the coffee/rolls/sausages meant for the crew have been used to bribe the army into silence, and your first day as a continuity girl has started.

What, in fact, is a continuity girl, and what does she do?

THE COMPLETE CONTINUITY GIRL

Dressed sensibly and warmly and hung about with the trappings of the
trade—clipboard, Polaroid camera, stopwatch, large canvas filming bag etc. etc. you
stand with eyes alert and poised pencil—the complete .... continuity girl.

11

Out of Sequence Shooting: 1

When a film is being made, it is not shot in a consecutive manner according to the story. That is to say, there is no progression from Scene 1 on Day 1 to Scene 25 on Day 25 or whenever shooting stops. It is generally shot out of sequence.

Take for example, the following story:

Story

Two guards are on the battlements of a castle. It is daytime. They see a dusty rider on the road, galloping towards them. One guard reaches for his gun. The rider suddenly reins in his horse and looks up at the castle. We see the rider's view of the castle.

Cut to a shot of a woman on board ship.

Back to the battlements where one guard is keeping watch on the rider and the other guard runs down some stairs to raise the alarm.

Cut again to the woman on the ship.

Cut to a room in the castle, full of drunken guards. They hear the alarm, leap up and rush from the room.

In order to plan when you are going to film each separate piece, this story would be broken down initially into scenes:

Scenes in story order

Scene	Subject	Int./Ext.	Time
1.	Castle battlements	Exterior	Day
2.	Dusty rider on road (seen from castle)	Exterior	Day
3.	Castle battlements		
4.	Dusty rider (from castle)		
5.	Rider's viewpoint of castle		
6.	Woman on ship	Exterior	Day
7.	Castle battlements. One guard exits Camera follows him down stairs		
8.	Battlements. Guard raises gun		
9.	Woman on ship		
10.	Mess room of castle	Interior	Day

SCENES IN STORY ORDER:

1. Castle battlements; 2. Dusty rider; 3. Battlements; 4. Rider; 5. Rider's POV of castle; 6. Woman on ship; 7. Battlements. Guard exits; 8. Guard raises gun; 9. Woman on ship; 10. Mess room of castle.

Out of Sequence Shooting: 2

Shooting in story order
If the filming were to take place in that order there would be a great deal of time-consuming trudging up and down flights of steps for the whole unit with all the equipment. It would also mean that all the artistes would be required for the whole of the time, which would be expensive, and that all the locations would have to be in the same area, which is unlikely. So the script is broken down into a shooting plan.

Shooting plan
The plan or schedule for filming is worked out bearing a number of things in mind.

Number of filming days
You might only have a specific number of days or weeks to film the story. You must try to fit the schedule into the requisite time allotted.

Position of locations
It takes time and a fair amount of organisation to move a film unit from place to place. Therefore it is better to film everything in location A before moving to location B, regardless of the order in the script.

Location availability
If a particular location is only available on certain dates, the rest of the locations will have to be arranged accordingly.

Actor's availability
As with locations, if a particular artiste is engaged, the schedule will have to fit in with their prior engagements depending on their importance to the production.

Shooting schedule

Day	Scene	Location	Interior/ exterior	Time	Characters
1	6	Ship	Ext.	Day	Woman
	9	Ship	Ext.	Day	Woman
2 a.m. p.m.		*Unit move to castle location*			
	1	Battlements of castle	Ext.	Day	2 guards
	3	Battlements of castle	Ext.	Day	2 guards
3	8	Battlements	Ext.	Day	1 guard
	7	Battlements and steps	Ext.	Day	2 guards
	2	Road (seen from battlements)	Ext.	Day	Rider and Horse
	4	Road (seen from battlements)	Ext.	Day	Rider and Horse
4	5	Road—LS castle	Ext.	Day	—
	10	Mess room	Int.	Day	20 soldiers

SHOOTING ORDER

A shooting order like this allows for the fact that the ship is at a different location from the castle. It uses the artists economically (the woman is only engaged for one day's filming), and the crew are not required to trudge up the steps to the battlements more than once, which allows a much faster shooting time.

Shots in Scenes Out of Order

A film is not only shot out of sequence, but the shots within each scene are generally not taken in order.

To save time
This happens for a number of reasons, all to do with wasting as little time as possible.

Usually only one camera is used in filming and it has to be moved when different angles are shot. It is far faster to take all the shots from one particular area, whether they are from the beginning, middle or end of the sequence. The camera does not have to be moved around too much between shots and the lighting needs minimum adjustment until a major re-light is required for a totally different angle. Also props do not have to be constantly moved here and there to keep them out of the way of the camera, the lights and the vast army of people hiding behind the camera.

PART OF A SET

This set has been lit and the camera set up to take shots from one angle.
Much time will be saved by taking all the shots needed from this area at
the same time, irrespective of where they occur in the scene, rather than moving
the equipment and lights from one side of the set to the other for each shot.

The Work of the Continuity Girl

A continuity girl is someone who provides a complete, written document of the shooting. It should be a very detailed and accurate yet very concise document. By concise, I mean that while a two page essay on each shot in a flowing literary style may be aesthetically pleasing to the continuity girl, it will be virtually useless as a working document, as no-one will have the time to plough through it for the information required.

Use of document: (A) to film unit
This document is of twofold use. The first use is to the film unit during shooting. As film is shot out of sequence it is obviously necessary to have some record, built up over the filming period, of what was actually shot, and also what each shot consisted of, in order to preserve continuity from shot to shot and scene to scene, irrespective of the shooting order.

This means that the closest attention must be paid to each shot, what happens in that shot, the smallest action noted, the relationship of the characters' actions to the spoken dialogue, the position of the props—in fact, as much of what the camera sees as possible must be written down for immediate and later reference.

Use of document: (B) to the film editor
The document also contains certain technical information which is of interest only to the film editor. He does not want to know what happens in each shot as he has only to run through the film to find out. But he is interested in the slate number, the shot description, the agreed take etc. (All these things will be discussed in detail later.)

Back to the original story
The continuity girl ensures that when the finished film is assembled and finally shown, it will flow in chronological order in a smooth way, and that continuity is preserved in action, sound, costume and props within each scene and from one scene to another.

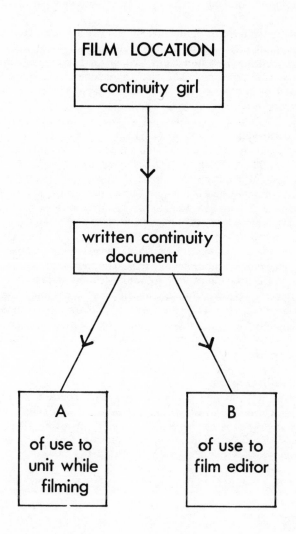

FILM CONTINUITY WORK

You provide a written record of the filming. This document is built up while filming takes place and is used as a reference while shooting. It is also of interest to the film editor for the technical information it contains.

How Do You Observe?

Before writing the continuity report, you must observe what is happening in each shot.

It is true to say that the more practice you have, the better you will become at observation, which is rather depressing for a beginner. But it is wrong to say 'observation' and leave it at that. One is observing things all the time—certain things make an impression and are retained *in some form or another* in the brain, while other things are seen, but in a generalised way, and no clear imprint is made.

Accurate observation

No two people retain the identical impression of a scene or event. Eye-witnesses at a road accident, for example, are notorious for the diversity of their reports of the same collision. But you can train yourself, or be trained, to observe specific things accurately. Some women workers on egg inspecting lines do nothing but watch eggs pass in front of a strong light, and they are trained to spot defects. Policemen are trained to give fast, accurate descriptions of people. They note certain things; height, build, colouring, clean-shaven or bearded, shape of head, clothes and so on. Likewise with continuity; there are specific things to observe and after a while it becomes second nature to note them.

Much of what you see throughout the day makes only the haziest imprint on the brain. You go into an unfamiliar room. Your eye is caught by a painting on the wall and you remember it afterwards with great clarity, while only having the vaguest impression of the rest of the surroundings.

Training in observation

When looking at continuity in filming you train yourself to notice not the random picture your eye happens to light upon and your brain register, but what is important for you to notice and record. That training comes very much from practice and experience but also from a number of other things.

20

SPOT THE DIFFERENCE

No two people retain an identical impression of a scene or event. Note the differences in the above pictures, which represent two eye-witness accounts of the same accident.

Thorough Knowledge of the Script

It is very important to get to know the script well before shooting. You should know, for example, where the scene you are about to shoot occurs in the story, and whether it has continuity with other scenes before or after.

Sometimes scenes occur which do not relate to any other. Then your job is easy.

Script interleaved with notes

The system I use is always to carry the script with me, in story order, with the pages of continuity notes of the scenes already shot interleaved with the script pages. Then, if having completed Scene 9 some weeks back which ends with an angry lady marching out camera right swinging a bag, when you come to Scene 10, in which the lady enters frame, you can check easily on the direction she enters, and which arm is swinging the bag (provided you noted it originally) by quickly referring back in your notes. Other people use other systems of course, and you will soon find the one which works best for you.

If you do not know the script fairly well, you have no chance of keeping accurate continuity between scenes, especially if you are working with a director who shoots at a rapid pace leaving you no time for more than an occasional quick glance at your script. By knowing the script, you can also save yourself much unnecessary work by being aware if a scene has no continuity with anything else. You can work that out the night before.

Working without a script

If you are working for someone who does not use a script, but develops a plot from improvisations, then it is very difficult to preserve any sort of continuity. A script may, in some cases, evolve during the weeks of rehearsals as the action and dialogue become fixed. If so, when you reach the filming stage you can then do continuity in the usual way.

If, however, a director has deliberately chosen to work without a script and does not allow any scene to become 'fixed', then there is very little you can do. If he does not want the restraints of working to a set script, then he will not want the restraints of a person doing continuity.

Only the director himself will then know how he wants the film cut together and all you can do is keep as extensive notes as possible. Also remember that continuity only exists *after* the first angle has been shot and accepted as a good take, so try to work things out from angle to angle and shot to shot. It might also help the editor if you write down how the action differs from shot to shot.

WORK OUT A FAST REFERENCE SYSTEM

Work out your own system to enable you to check continuity points quickly from scene to scene.

When shooting the second scene (shown above as the second picture) you must be able to check the important points quickly—how the lady is dressed and which way she should enter frame.

Coverage Planned

After getting to know the script, try to find out the director's plans for coverage of a scene.

Important junctions
If you know where the important junctions for cuts will be, you can pay particular attention to the continuity at those points.

The director, of course, may not have any plans, except, one assumes, in his head.

Circulated shot lists
Almost every director I have worked with has started filming in an incredibly efficient way by having lists of their proposed shots circulated to the unit. After a few days the unit thank you profusely for these lists, fold them up neatly and put them away 'in a safe place', never to be looked at again, and the director then confines his lists to himself and you.

After two weeks or so of filming even these lists, which have become vaguer day by day, cease, and you must find other ways of determining what sort of shot is being planned.

Film shooting script
There are occasions, however, when you might find yourself working for a very well organised director, one who plans well in advance exactly what he is going to shoot and works out each angle with meticulous care. You should, of course, think yourself very lucky to be working for such a paragon—but do watch out for one thing.

He might well have written a 'film shooting script'—sometimes backed up by extensive diagrams showing exactly where the camera and artistes will be placed. This shooting script can be of unbelievable complexity with boxes for the shot number, the order of shooting, the camera position, an empty space for you to mark in the slate number and then the body of the script neatly squared round for each shot. Such a script can be of immense help in giving a very good idea of what the director *intends* to do, but do beware of following it too slavishly as it may well differ quite considerably from what he *actually* does on the day of filming. Your job is to note down what actually happened and not what your director's intentions were some five weeks or even five days before the shooting.

THE DIRECTOR'S PLANS

There are a number of ways of finding out how the director plans to cover
the script.

How to Keep Informed

Stick by the director
If you stick to the director and cameraman like a limpet you won't miss out when angles are being discussed, or even when quick shots are being taken, unbeknown to the rest of the unit.

Master shot then cutaways
It is fairly safe to assume that the first shot of a particular scene will be the master or establishing shot, and the rest of the coverage will follow. But this is by no means always the case, and I have known directors to start with shooting the two-shots and singles and ended by shooting the master; this is usually done with good reason.

Position of the zoom handle
The camera operator may be using a zoom lens by which he can adjust the magnification of the picture or, in other words, the amount of the scene that is included in the shot. Although you are not looking through the viewfinder yourself, you can always judge what he is seeing by the position of the zoom handle which will tell you whether the shot is wide or close. But do find out first whether the wide angle setting is at the top or bottom of the lens, as they vary.

Keep close behind camera
Always stand as close behind the camera as possible. You can't describe a shot accurately if you are five feet away from the camera position, as you are seeing everything from a different angle. Do not set yourself up with a little folding table and camp stool some way away from all the activity. You may be comfortable, but you'll be wildly inaccurate in your notes.

Look through the viewfinder
No cameraman will object if you ask to look through the camera viewfinder. You should do so at rehearsals to find out where the edge of frame or area of the picture seen by the camera, is and what precisely is included in the shot. (You can also check whether it contains things like scripts, props and unwanted other miscellanea which have no place in the set.) But remember that looking through the viewfinder during rehearsal does not give you any indication of change of focal length during a shot if the camera is using a zoom lens.

You can always ask
Finally, if all else fails, you can always ask the director or the camera operator, but do not make a habit of it, otherwise you will be labelled a liability.

KEEP CLOSE TO THE CAMERA

By keeping as near the director and cameraman as possible you not only keep abreast of what angles are being discussed and taken, but are also in a position to describe the shots more accurately.

27

Know What to Observe: 1

Good continuity is not *just* being good at observation. It is knowing what is important to observe.

Once you know what the shot is you can observe as necessary.

Close shots
It really is rather a wasted exercise giving detailed information about the clothes an actor is wearing when a large close-up of the face is being shot. It is also unnecessary to worry too much about the position of the props in such a close-up, unless the props are in frame or brought into frame, i.e. a close-up of someone drinking or a cigarette being brought up to the lips.

Mid shots
Be aware of *exactly* what is in shot. For example, someone is reading a book and turning the pages over frequently. In a close-up, all you see is a face, frowning with concentration; in a wide shot you see the whole action with the book in shot. In a mid shot, even though the book itself is not visible do not ignore the operation of turning over the pages, because the upper arm and shoulder movements will be noticeable.

Wide shots
In a very wide shot, it isn't necessary to be as observant of the minute details of actions and props as in the closer shots. In a wide shot of a pub interior with many actors sitting and standing with their drinks, the exact levels of the drink are unimportant, as long as something is in their glasses.

Very long shots
In a very long shot it might prove to be immaterial whether or not there is any drink at all, as it is impossible even to see the glass.

A

B

Close shots
Only worry about the clothes or
props when these are in frame
(A,B).

C

D

Mid shots
It is important to know exactly
what is in shot.
All you see in the close-up is the
face (C).
In the wide shot you see all the
action (D).
In the mid shot you will see the
upper arm movement as the
pages are turned over (E).

E

F

G

Wide shots
You do not have to be as
observant of the minute details
in this busy station shot (F).

Very long shot
In this long shot it is just
possible to see the three
figures—let alone details of
clothing and props (G,H).

H

29

Know What to Observe: 2

It is generally true to say that the more that is happening in a shot, the less continuity matters. But in a constrained, intimate situation, every head turn counts.

Intimate situations

Two characters are having a quiet *tête-à-tête* over dinner. They are eating, and sometimes talking, but nothing much is happening visually. In such a situation it is most important to be accurate about all the actions, even head nods and slight gestures, particularly where the director has planned to cover the scene with complementary two-shots (see page 42). In these shots both characters are in vision all the time and it is only possible to cut from one to the other when the dialogue and action match exactly on each shot.

If the director has planned a coverage of single shots on each person, the action is not so critical as most of it is out of view. The props also are of great importance in such a scene.

The opposite extreme to an intimate situation in terms of observing detail for continuity would be a fight sequence, including a large number of people and props. It would be impossible to notice everything, especially head nods, in a situation with such violent activity. But in this kind of set up you should note carefully what the principal actors are doing and try to keep track of their relationship with other groups.

For instance, in the early part of a scene two principals may be fighting with each other in the thick of other extras. In the latter part of the same scene the principals are still fighting it out, but the extras have cleared save for a group on camera right. So remember that.

Also, be aware of clothes becoming disarranged during a fight and possible make-up requirements, like blood and bruising, that may have continuity with other shots and scenes in the film.

1.   In a scene with little action, every detail of continuity is important.

These two complementary 2-shots will only cut together if continuity matches exactly in every detail.

2.   But in a scene with a lot of action, accuracy over every detail is not so vital.

Just pay attention to the principal characters and have a general idea what else is happening in the shot.

31

Rehearsals and Actors

Rehearsals are vitally important as they provide you with your only opportunity of writing down all the information you need. You will never be able to do the job properly if you ignore the rehearsals and only pay attention during the actual take.

The reason is that there is so much you need to notice in any shot that you can only build up a complete picture bit by bit. Rehearsals afford you the opportunity to do this. For example, during the first rehearsal of a scene, you may not be able to write down the action, but you can at least make a note of the actor's costume. You can also take a Polaroid or other instant picture or draw a diagram of the basic set and the approximate camera position. At the next rehearsal you can note down a bit more—perhaps the overall action, and slowly you will find that you have built up more and more information until you can concentrate entirely on the specific actions and props. Things will be bound to change from one rehearsal to another, but it is far simpler to alter your notes accordingly as and when the changes happen than it is to start writing from scratch during a take. In fact during a take you should not be writing at all, just watching. Leave writing until the take is over.

Problems with actors

If an actor is good with props and naturally does the same action at the same time and with the same bit of dialogue you can stop worrying about him, except to remind him of movements when the master shot was taken some time back, or in scenes where the action is complicated.

If an actor is not consistent, watch him or her like a hawk. Don't worry during the rehearsals, but write down the exact movements during a take, so that you can go over them with him later for cutaways—extra shots of him to be inserted in the main action, if needed. Do not let anyone else tell him what he did and when. He will only get confused between your advice and everyone else's. You get in first. It's your job.

The difficult actor

Watch out for the 'difficult' actor. He tends to be terribly nervous and unsure of his actions. He will constantly come up to you to ask anxiously what he did with his left hand in the last take, and he will probably worry incessantly about everything. Always have an answer ready. Maybe you did not notice what he did with his left hand. Perhaps it was not even in shot—but never let him know that you have not recorded his every move, in or out of vision. He needs reassurance and will stop worrying only when he feels he can rely on you. You need to keep a careful eye on him for another reason as well; he will argue to the end if he thinks you are wrong about something.

Some actors are good with
props . . .

. . . and some have to be
watched carefully.

33

Your Role Within the Unit

As you have seen from the preceding sections, your job is a pretty important one.

Avoid being sidetracked
Never be sidetracked into doing anything else when shooting is in progress. Your job is to be where the action is, literally. Continuity implicitly requires you to be there and give your constant attention *all* the time. This does not apply in the feature industry where the job of continuity girl is clearly defined, but in television you must be clear about your role, as so many other aspects are involved.

Never leave the set and always try to be in a position where you can clearly see all the action. This is usually possible even if it means crouching under the camera.

Continuity is your responsibility
You will find during your first day that everyone knows about continuity. The camera operator says the glass was filled to the brim and positioned on the table. The second assistant insists that the glass was only half full and positioned on the other side of the table. The designer asserts that he left the glass empty on the sideboard and the first assistant swears that there was no glass at all. You *know* that the glass was actually full and in the actor's hand at the relevant moment. (The actor, by the way, remains uncommitted.)

That kind of situation must be stopped before long and involved discussions take place. That is not to imply in any way that no one other than you can be correct about points of continuity. But you are in the unique position of having nothing to do other than watch the action, and if you cannot be more accurate than, say, the second assistant, who might have spent the greater part of the shot stuck behind a bush waiting to give an artist his cue, then you really should not be doing the job.

Continuity is not an abstract, academic game in 'getting it right', whereby you score a point everytime you notice something. It is *what* you notice that is important and, conversely, the art lies in knowing what you need not bother to notice. So do not be perturbed when well-meaning members of the crew come up to you and say, 'Didn't you notice that Fanny's wig was askew during that take?' so long as you *know* that a close up of Fanny's left foot was being shot.

ALWAYS WATCH THE ACTION

Continuity is your responsibility. Don't ever be sidetracked when shooting is taking place.

Always try to be in a position where you can see all the action even if it means crouching under the camera.

35

Making Mistakes

You will of course make mistakes. But a large part of the job is that of having confidence in your accuracy, because then you can get the confidence of the unit and time wasting arguments do not arise. One small addition. If you only *think* you are right in a particular situation, act as if you are sure, because it is fairly safe to say that if you have not noticed, neither will anyone else.

What to do over a mistake
If you or an artiste makes a mistake, and you are immediately aware of it, you can always quietly tell the director and ask for a re-take. Occasionally a director will not re-take for continuity. In that case there is little you can do, except take the rather drastic and ill-advised action of walking into shot, smiling broadly and saying 'Hello Ma'. But after such action you might well find yourself off the set and possibly off the film.

If you make an error in a scene already shot and the continuity will affect another scene there are numerous ways of getting round the problem of matching the two scenes. The dialogue could be slightly altered, the first shot for the next scene changed, or even, as happened on the first film I worked on, a new scene written in to overcome a costume error.

RE-TAKES FOR CONTINUITY

Except for walking into shot and ruining the take there is little you can do
if a director will not re-take for continuity. In such a situation all you *can*
do is point out the necessity for a re-take and then keep quiet.

What Do You Observe?

To say that you should observe 'everything' is not much use and not strictly accurate. You could not do that anyway. It is your job to provide a written record of the shooting and to preserve continuity from one sequence to another and within each sequence in the process.

Shot description
An accurate description of the shot is the first essential. After this you note where in the sequence the shot begins and ends. You may not notice much of the middle of the shot but at least there is a reasonable chance that the two shots will cut together. Note particularly the way actors enter and leave frame. When referring to exits and entrances you should do so from your viewpoint, which is also that of the camera and the audience. For example, 'Fred enters frame camera left and exits bottom of frame right.'

But in order to write down an accurate shot description, you need to know the correct terminology and be consistent in your use of it.

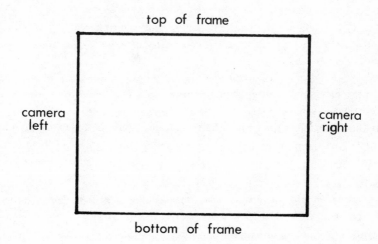

top of frame

camera
left

camera
right

bottom of frame

EXITS AND ENTRANCES

A point to remember is that when referring to entrances and exits always do
so from your (also the camera and audience) viewpoint.

How to Describe Shots

W/A This is a wide-angle shot. A wide-angle shot takes in a wide area of the scene in front of the camera. It is often called 'the master' or 'establishing' shot of the scene because of the tradition of setting the scene.

LS Long shot. One in which the subject occupies a relatively small part of the picture.

3-s Three shot. A shot containing three central characters.

2-s Two shot. A shot containing two central characters.

2-s fav. X A shot with two people—the camera favours one person more than the other.

O/S 2-s Over-the-shoulder two shot. Two people are seen in the shot but the camera is looking at one of them over the shoulder of the other.

MS Mid shot. A scene at normal viewing distance. In the case of the human subject the camera frame cuts the figure just below the waist.

MCU Medium close up. The camera frame cuts figures at chest level.

CU Close up. The camera frame cuts the subject just below the neck.

BCU Big close up. The face fills the screen.

X's POV X's point of view shot. The camera is X and sees as if from his point of view.

Panning Camera turns from one side to the other, pivoting horizontally on an axis, either right to left or left to right.

Tilting Camera pivoting vertically on an axis, tilting up or tilting down.

Tracking (also trucking or dollying) Camera is physically moved forward or back, towards or away from the subject. It may be held in the operator's hand to do this or is placed on a dolly. This is like a trolley on wheels and runs along specially laid tracks.

Crabbing The camera is physically moved crabwise or sideways to the direction of view, again either hand-held or on a dolly.

H/A High angle. The camera is above the action and looking down on it.

L/A Low angle. The camera is below the action and looking up.

Z/I Zoom in. The camera is not moved but the focal length of the lens is altered. This magnifies the subject without changing the perspective of the scene (as opposed to a track where the camera moves towards the subject and the perspective changes as if you were walking towards it.)

Z/O Zoom out. The lens is adjusted in the reverse direction from the above.

DESCRIPTION OF SHOTS

1. Wide angle (W/A). 2. Long shot (LS). 3. Three shot (3-s). 4. Two shot (2-s). 5. Two shot favouring X (2-s fav. X). 6. Over the shoulder two shot favouring Y (o/s 2-s fav. Y). 7. Mid shot (MS). 8. Medium close-up (MCU). 9. Close-up (CU). 10. Big close-up (BCU). 11. High angle (H/A). 12. Low angle (L/A). 13. Tracking (the camera is mounted on a dolly and physically moved). 14. Panning (the camera turns from one side to the other). 15. Tilting (the camera moves up and down).

Other Terms Used to Describe Shots

C/A (Cutaway)
This can apply to any shot that is not a master; for example, a close up. Such a shot often emphasizes or highlights a particular aspect of events when it is inserted in the main action.

Safety measure
Cutaways are also used as a safety measure. For example: a woman is telling a long story. Several cutaway shots are taken of her audience. The woman's story can then either be shortened by cutting away to the audience, or the cutaways can be used for dramatic effect—to build up atmosphere, heighten tension and generally give pace to a scene.

Under- and over-cranking
On TV, film is shot and projected at a standard rate of 25 frames per second (feature films are projected at 24 fps). That is to say, 25 separate little pictures pass in succession to give the illusion of movement. Any departure from this standard speed in either shooting or projecting the film alters the rate of the action. Under-cranking is a term to denote shooting at less than the standard projection speed; over-cranking for greater than that speed. The 'cranking' part of the term originates from the days when cameras were cranked by hand. Under-cranking and projecting at the normal rate speeds up the action whereas over-cranking slows it down on projection. If a car moving at 30 mph is filmed by under-cranking at 12 fps, (ie roughly half the normal rate) it will appear on the screen to be moving at just over 60 mph. If, on the other hand the camera is over-cranking at 50 fps on projection, the car will appear to travel at only 15 mph. (This is impossible with sync sound shots.)

Matte shot
This is a shot in which a mask is inserted in the camera to achieve a particular effect blanking out a part of the picture at the time of shooting, such as in the shape of keyholes, binoculars etc.

Overlay shot
This is filmed material taken for use in a subsequent filming or studio operation, and not containing the complete action. An overlay shot is used later in an electronic studio with action taking place around it, ie the countryside passing the windows of a car might be filmed on location and the car and the actors set up in the studio. The live action and the projected background image are then combined in the shot.

BP shot
A BP (or back projection) shot is used in the same way except that the final result is filmed rather than electronically recorded. BP is always shot on 35mm film material.

42

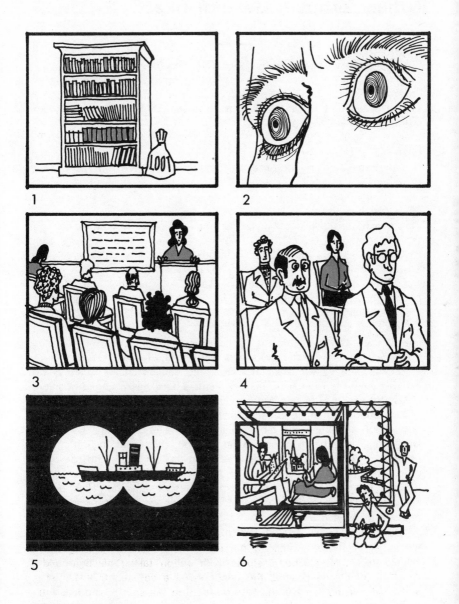

OTHER TERMS USED

1. Cutaway from W/A of guilty man looking towards bookcase. 2. Cutaway from a close up of a woman screaming. 3. A woman is talking to an audience . . . 4. . . . a cutaway is taken of the audience to use: (a) to shorten the woman's chat. (b) for dramatic effect. 5. A matte gives a particular effect, eg: binoculars. 6. A set using back projection.

Other Terms in General Use

Coverage
The number of different camera angles used to 'cover' one scene.

OOV
Out of vision; out of the view of the camera. Might relate to an actor speaking his lines out of vision.

OOF
Out of frame. (Also 'out of film'). An actor exits OOF R or L (out of frame right or left).

Crossing the line
This term is best illustrated by means of a diagram. A train is passing through a station. The camera on Platform 1 sees a train entering from the left and exiting right. The camera on Platform 2 sees the *same train* entering from the right and exiting left. If two shots were taken of the same train—one from each platform—and joined together one after the other, the result would be as if the train had suddenly and dramatically changed direction.

You have to imagine that the direction of movement is an invisible line. If the camera crosses this line and so faces the subject from the opposite side, the direction of movement appears to be reversed.

Because the viewer sees only what the camera shows, there is no external evidence to indicate that the camera itself has changed position, unless the film makes this apparent in some way.

Take another example not this time involving a moving subject. Two men A & B are sitting at a table playing cards. The camera in the master shot establishes that A is seated on the left and B on the right. Any other shot in that scene must feature A on the left and B on the right, otherwise it appears that A and B have changed places at the table. If for a subsequent shot the camera crosses an imaginary line drawn along the axis of these two people, then B appears on the left of the frame, and A on the right.

This should never happen, except when: 1. A tracking shot which moves round the table, *takes* the viewer over the line and through to a new angle, or; 2. With the introduction of a third character, C, who walks round the table. Shots can then be taken from C's point of view if he has first been seen to walk round the table in the master shot.

Direct reverse
A direct reverse shot is one in which the camera moves to the far side of the subject and directly faces the position it held in the previous shot. All the rules about crossing the line are broken but it works.

44

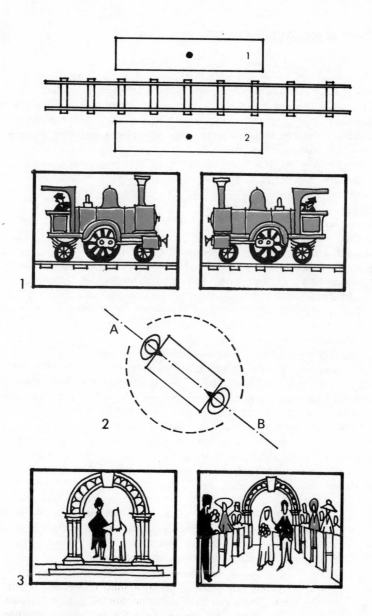

CROSSING THE LINE

1. The shot of the train taken from Platform 1 and the shot from Platform
   2 show the same train apparently travelling in opposite directions.
2. If the invisible line is crossed, A would be sitting where B is.
3. This direct reverse works. Why? They have their backs to the camera and
   the bride is on the right. Inside the church the next shot shows them facing
   the camera. Their positions are reversed.

The Basics: Props

Ask anyone not connected with filming—and a good many people who are—what they immediately think of when the term 'continuity in film' is mentioned. Many believe it is a question of avoiding an accidental total change of costume from one shot to the next, or props appearing in different places from shot to shot, or things suddenly disappearing ... and so on.

There is a good deal more to continuity than maintaining consistency in costume and props, but those are often the most noticeable.

Props

First note the general position of props, not only dressing props like candles which are alight, but the general dressing of the set. Take a Polaroid shot of the set or draw a diagram. This is useful if you are working for several days on the same set, or for reference in the case of a shot being retaken when you have to remember how everything was arranged.

Then, pay particular attention to props which are used in the course of the action.

Note when an artiste uses these props, which hand they use and at precisely what point in the dialogue these actions occur.

For example: an actor is sitting at a table alternately drinking a glass of wine, eating a meal and holding an earnest conversation waving the wine glass or fork in the air. Write down when he sips the wine, when he eats, when he waves the utensils in the air and at what point in the script. Also do not forget the level of wine in the glass and the amount of food on the plate, for cutaways. After the master shot you may do a 2-shot from the start of the scene. If, at the start of the master the glass was full, make sure it is refilled before starting the 2-shot.

Other points to notice are props which are not used by the actor but are there as dressing. On the table there may be a candle, which has been alight from the beginning. Suppose in the master shot the candle was tall and new, remember not to let it burn down to a tiny stump by the time the cutaways are done.

PROPS

Note the general position of the props by drawing a diagram or taking a Polaroid
photograph, but only worry about the props that will be used in the action.

The Basics: Costume

More arguments and problems seem to arise over costume than almost anything else, but it is really only a matter of working things out intelligently in advance.

The costume designer will have worked out which scenes have continuity of costume with which. But things often happen in the course of the shooting which might bring about changes in the costume in a later scene. For example, an actor might take off his coat in the middle of one scene, and that scene has continuity with another one. Only you would be aware of these points.

Take a Polaroid
At the start of filming line all your artistes up and take Polaroid shots of them. Likewise, when they change into another costume. It is most advisable to take colour Polaroid pictures, as shirts etc. can look very similar in black and white. That point might seem so obvious that it's not worth making, but it has been known to cause confusion on more than one occasion.

Write it down
Always write down exactly what the artiste is wearing at the start of every new scene, and if there is any change within a scene. It might seem tedious, but it will prove its worth at least once within the first week of shooting.

Do not just write down the bare minimum: 'Mrs Bold: hat, coat, dress' does not convey very much information. Is the coat done up or undone? How far is it done up—all the way? What sort of dress is she wearing? What colour? Is the hat on her head or in her hand? What about her shoes? Does she have any accessories like handbag, gloves etc.?

My first continuity error was over a scarf that was being worn in one scene and not in the next. My second was over a pair of wellington boots. No one may notice these mistakes, or they might achieve unwelcome fame. With a little care and trouble you need never make them.

Make a note or take a Polaroid photograph of costume. You can easily mislay a few items of clothing—especially with period costume.

Not only has this soldier lost his hat—he has also lost his bag, his sword, and the top of his bayonet. Its obvious when the pictures are placed together as these are, but you could easily make the same mistake in the real situation and you had not made copious notes or taken a photograph.

49

Continuity of Action

Some of the least obvious aspects of continuity are no less important than those already discussed. But they are often overlooked because thay are not often apparent in the finished film. The reason they are not apparent is usually because the film editor has found a way round the mistakes in one way or another, but in doing so, the artistic role of the film editing process may have been severely limited. Such errors put an unnecessary and time-consuming burden on the editor.

Let us examine these aspects of continuity by starting with the simplest—continuity of action.

Example 1: A girl walks across a bridge, putting her coat on in the process.

The director has planned two camera angles on this action: one from the bank, with the girl walking away from the camera, and the other from the opposite bank, with the girl walking towards the camera. The cut from one camera angle to the other takes place when the girl is somewhere on the bridge.

Suppose in shooting these two angles, there was an error of continuity in the action of putting on the coat. When the girl put on the coat in the second shot, she was in a different position on the bridge from when she did this in the first shot.

If those shots were then cut and joined together at the logical place, where the director had planned it, the result would show a jump in the action—a jump cut.

It is possible in that situation for the editor to 'cover up' this error of continuity by cutting earlier or later. But that would not give as smooth a cut as if the action had been repeated correctly in the second shot. In other words, the cut had to be made where it was mechanically possible and not in the way that was most suitable dramatically.

Example 2: A man opens a door with a key. He enters and closes the door behind him.

There are two camera angles—one on each side of the door. The second angle is taken much later and as the action with the key has been shot on the first angle, the door is set for the man to just push it open for the second shot. On that angle he pushes the door open and walks in and everyone accepts the take. *But he uses a different hand on the door* and the film editor is faced with the same problem as before.

CONTINUITY OF ACTION

A

B

1st angle

C

2nd angle
Note that the coat is put on in a different place in the bridge. It would not cut together with the first angle

This would have been the correct place for putting the coat on

D

E

1st angle
Man approaches door (outside) (D).

F

G

2nd angle
From the other side of the door (inside) (E,F).
Continuity of the hands differs from the first angle. These shots would not cut together

The position of the hands are correct in this shot (G).

51

Continuity of Action and Dialogue

What happens when there is dialogue as well?

Example 1: A presenter of a programme is coming to the end of a long piece spoken 'to camera'. He moves off, out of frame *after* saying "We pass on to the next exhibit". The second angle is a wide exit shot, and he repeats the end of his piece and then moves off. But he starts to move off *on* the words "We pass on . . .".

If those two shots were cut together there would either be a loss of action (a jump cut), or double dialogue: "We pass on" on the first angle, and again "We pass on" repeated on the second angle.

In such a case the editor would either use the ugly jump cut, or stay on one shot only. He obviously cannot repeat the dialogue. Either way it spoils the intended effect and, if only one shot is used, makes the shooting of the second shot totally pointless. One often sees that a jump cut has been used to get over this type of error. But it is quite wrong to force the editor into using such a jarring effect because of sloppy continuity.

To make the relationship of action to dialogue absolutely clear, take this well-known nursery rhyme:

Example 2: A girl is walking along, swinging a shoulder bag and reciting:
   "Mary had a little lamb,
   Its fleece was white as snow.
   And everywhere that Mary went
   The lamb was sure to go."
On the first angle she places the bag on her shoulder *after* saying: "Its fleece was white as snow".

But on the second angle she places the bag on her shoulder *before* saying: "Its fleece was white as snow".

When those shots are cut together there is either a sudden jump in the action—from the girl with the bag in her hand, to the girl with the bag on her shoulder, or the action is perfect and the dialogue is as follows:

First angle
"Mary had a little lamb
Its fleece was white as snow"

Second angle
"Its fleece was white as snow,
And everywhere that Mary went
The lamb was sure to go".

Mary had a little lamb

Its fleece was white as snow

And everywhere that Mary went

The lamb was sure to go.

ACTION AND DIALOGUE

On the first angle the girl places the bag on her shoulder *after* saying 'Its fleece was white as snow' and on the second angle she places it on her shoulder *before* saying the same dialogue.

If those shots are cut together there will either be a jump in the action, or double dialogue.

Drama Situations

It is not often, however, that you have only one character to concentrate on. Things get more complicated as more characters are involved.

Example: A man is sitting on a seat. A girl enters frame—she walks up to the man. She says "Hello". The man replies likewise. He gets up and they exit.

That could hardly be simpler. But endless variations of that simple scene are possible.

Does the girl stop *before* she speaks, *as* she speaks, or not at all? Where does she stop?

When does the man get up?

Does he speak from the seat, on the rise, or standing?

What is the relationship of the man and the girl as she speaks/as he speaks/as he rises?

And so on.

If that simple scene were shot from two angles with both characters in shot in each angle, the continuity has to match exactly on each angle.

first angle   second angle

THE SIMPLE DRAMA SCENE

On each angle the action in relation to the dialogue must match exactly, otherwise the shots 1, 2, 3 will not cut together.

The Complete Scene

We have now looked at the different ingredients to observe for continuity—action, dialogue, props and costume. Now we shall put them all together in the following scene:

Fred and Mabel
Scene 1: Kitchen: day
MABEL IS PREPARING AN APPLE PIE.
FRED COMES IN FROM THE GARDEN AND RUSHES OVER TO THE SINK. HE TURNS ON THE TAP AND HOLDS HIS HAND UNDER THE STREAM OF WATER.
MABEL GOES OVER TO HIM.

MABEL: Fred, Fred, what's happened?

MABEL EXAMINES HIS HURT HAND

MABEL: How on earth did you do that?

FRED: The bloody adjuster stuck on the lawn mower.

MABEL: You've got dirt in it.

SHE PUTS HIS HAND BACK UNDER THE TAP.

MABEL: I'll get you a plaster.

SHE GOES TO THE CUPBOARD AND GETS OUT A TIN OF DRESSINGS

MABEL: Do you want some antiseptic on it?

FRED: No, don't bother.

MABEL TAKES A TOWEL AND GIVES IT TO FRED. HE DRIES HIS HAND ON IT.

FRED: Thanks, love.

MABEL STICKS DRESSING ON FRED'S FINGER. HE WINCES.

MABEL: Did I hurt you?

FRED: No. It's just a bit sore. (PAUSE) Right. I'll finish the lawn.

BOTH GO TO THE BACK DOOR.

FRED: What time's lunch?

MABEL: Is half an hour all right?

FRED: Fine. Give me a shout.

HE KISSES HER AND GOES OUT.

Scene 2: Garden: day
FRED COMES OUT OF THE HOUSE AND WALKS TO LAWN MOWER . . .

THE COMPLETE SCENE

The scene is set for Fred and Mabel.

57

Fred and Mabel: Coverage Planned

The director has planned the following shots for Scene 1 and he has further planned to shoot them in this order:

1. Wide angle of whole scene (master)
2. Tight 2-s Fred and Mabel at sink
3. MCU tap and hand
4. CU dressing going on to finger
5. CU Fred wincing
6. MCU cupboard—tin being removed
7. MS Mabel looking pleased with pie
8. 2-s Fred and Mabel at door

Without being able to show the action in the master shot, I shall try to describe it as fully as possible. When actually doing the continuity for the master, you should have written or noticed as much of the following as possible. There are some obvious pitfalls and important things to notice for the other angles and I have mentioned these where necessary.

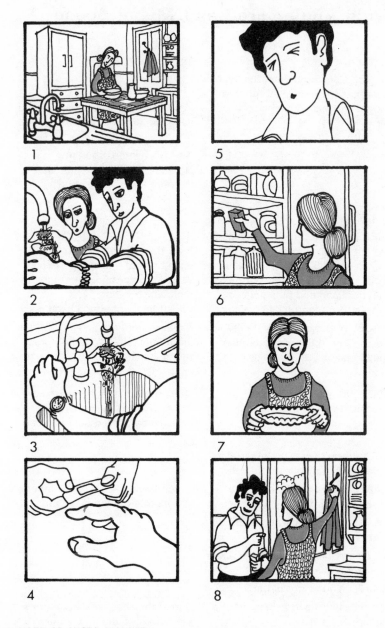

NUMBER OF SHOTS PLANNED

1. Wide angle (W/A). 2. Tight two shot (Tight 2-s). 3. Medium close-up tap and hand (MCU tap and hand). 4. Close-up plaster (CU plaster). 5. Close-up Fred (CU Fred). 6. Medium close-up cupboard (MCU cupboard). 7. Mid-shot Mabel (MS Mabel). 8. Two shot at door (2-s at door).

Wide Angle: Fred and Mabel Scene: 1

Action and sound

Important to observe

MABEL standing behind the kitchen table puts the last thumb print in the pie and stands back to admire her work.

How does she stand back? Wiping hands on apron or what?

She turns to the oven and opens the
door.

Which way does she turn?
Note the oven door action. Is the door left open or shut?

She turns back to table and picks up pie.

FRED comes in through back door (which is closed to start), he leaves it open, crosses behind Mabel and dashes to sink. He turns on the tap with left hand and puts finger of right hand under the jet of water.

Back door closed to start—left open by Fred—keep an eye on it
Which tap does Fred turn on and with which hand?
Which finger of which hand is cut?

MABEL puts pie back on table—closes door of the oven with her knee in passing and hurries over to Fred.

Pie does not figure again, but it is left on the table so do not forget that it is there.

Note oven door action

MABEL: Fred, Fred, what's happened?

Does she say that line on the move or when she is by Fred's side? Which side of Fred does she end up on?

FRED doesn't answer. Just swears under his breath.

MABEL is now at the sink. She takes his right hand with her left.

Which hand takes which? Important to note that the tap is left running.

MABEL: How on earth did you do that?

FRED: The bloody adjuster stuck on the lawn mower.

MABEL: You've got dirt in it.

She sticks his hand back under the tap.

During the above dialogue, does she hold his hand all the time? Does she bring his hand up to her face to look closely at the wound, or bend down to look. When *exactly* does she stick his hand back under the tap?

Action and sound (cont)

MABEL : I'll get you a dressing.

She crosses to the cupboard—opens the door (right hand to open it)—takes out tin of dressings (with right hand)—transfers tin to her left and says:

MABEL : Do you want some antiseptic on it?

FRED : No, don't bother.

Important to observe (cont)

Note all her actions at the cupboard—which hand does what. N.B. There is a bottle of antiseptic in the cupboard. Make sure it is still there for the cutaways.

Does she say that line while transferring the tin to left hand or after?

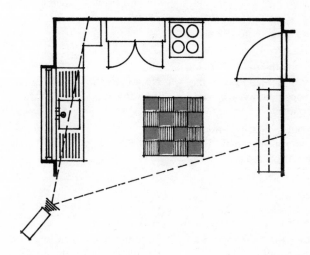

Plan view of kitchen with camera position showing complete scene as per page 59.

Wide Angle: Fred and Mabel Scene: 2

Action and sound	Important to observe
MABEL leaves the cupboard door open—moves to the back door—half closes it and with her right hand picks up a towel from a hook on the back.	Note that cupboard door. I said to keep an eye on the back door.
She moves forward to the sink. FRED turns off the tap with his left hand and takes the towel from Mabel also with his left hand.	Tap action. At what point does Fred turn it off? ie: what is Mabel doing then? Which hand does he turn it off with and does he take the towel before or after turning off the tap and with which hand?
FRED starts gingerly to dry his cut finger.	
MABEL opens the tin of dressings with her right hand and puts the lid down (upside down) on the draining board.	Note the action—particularly with the lid.
She takes out a dressing and puts the tin down on the draining board beside the lid (on the right side).	
FRED: Thanks love.	When does Fred speak? Is Mabel still taking the lid off the tin, or the dressing out of the tin or what?
FRED throws the towel down on the draining board.	Note that Fred speaks and then throws the towel down. Also note where it lands.
MABEL unpeels the dressing from its backing and places it on Fred's finger. Fred turns his head away and winces.	Does she use both hands to place the dressing on his finger? Note the way Fred's head turns to wince.
MABEL: Did I hurt you?	Note that she speaks before he turns his head back.
FRED turns his head back.	
FRED: No, it's just a bit sore.	
MABEL takes her hands away.	Note when she removes her hands.
FRED: Right. I'll finish the lawn.	

Action and sound (cont)	*Important to observe* (cont)
MABEL picks up the towel with her left hand and moves to the door.	Note the hand.
FRED picks up the lid of the dressings tin and places it on the box—picks up the box with left hand and moves to the door.	Note the hand, also that Mabel moved to door before Fred.
MABEL hangs the towel up at the door—FRED moves over to her with the tin which he hands over (his left hand to her right).	Still do not forget the back door. Note the hand action.
FRED: What time's lunch?	
MABEL: Is half an hour all right?	
FRED: Fine. Give me a shout.	Do not forget that during the dialogue Mabel is holding the tin.
FRED kisses her. He pulls open the door and goes out.	Kisses her after the dialogue. Note. You see about the door?

N.B. When you come to do the scene directly following this one, which is Exterior, Garden, you will of course know that Fred must have a dressing on the relevant finger of his right hand, and that the back door is slightly open, at the start of the shot, before Fred comes out!

Remaining Coverage : Fred and Mabel Sc. 1

Having shot the master, the director goes on to shoot the rest of the coverage. This is your first test.

2-s Fred and Mabel at sink

From Fred turning on the tap—putting his hand under the water—you will remember which tap and which hand—Mabel comes up to him—she examines his hand—chat—tap still running—she replaces his hand under the tap—she exits frame (do you know which way)—chat with her out of vision—she returns with towel and tin (in which hands)—Fred turns off tap and takes towel—he dries his hand. Mabel meanwhile goes through the same actions as the master opening the tin. Fred puts the towel on the draining board. Mabel places dressing on Fred's finger. Fred turns his head away (which way?) and winces. Mabel speaks—Fred turns back to her and speaks—Mabel takes her hand away. Fred says he will finish the lawn. Mabel takes the towel and exits. Fred does his action with the tin of dressings and also exits.

MCU tap and hand

Hand in to tap—turns on water (which tap and which hand). The finger, (suitably wounded) is placed under the water.

CU dressing going on finger

Mabel's hand holding dressing—places it on Fred's outstretched finger and presses firmly into place. (Make sure that Fred's finger is no longer wet, as he has just dried it with a towel.)

CU Fred wincing

Fred turns his head and winces. Mabel says her line out of vision and Fred turns back.

OTHER SHOTS PLANNED

Tight two shot (Tight 2-s)

Medium close-up tap
and hand (MCU tap and hand)

Close-up plaster (CU plaster)

Close-up Fred (CU Fred)

Remaining Coverage : Fred and Mabel Sc. 2

MCU cupboard
The cupboard door is shut to start. Mabel's right hand opens the door and reveals a tin of dressings and a bottle of antiseptic (both of which have been replaced after the W/A)—her right hand takes the bottle, then replaces it and takes tin of dressings—the cupboard door is left open and she moves her hand away.

MS Mabel looking pleased with the pie
As you noted on the master that she rubs her hands on the front of her apron, she can repeat that action. You also noted the way she turned to the oven, and that she left the pie on the table and did not take it with her.

2-s Fred and Mabel at door
Mabel goes to back door (holding the towel in left hand). The back door is half closed. She hangs the towel on the back. Fred enters from foreground to form a two-shot (Fred's finger is dressed and he carries the tin with him in his left hand). He hands tin to Mabel—chat—he kisses her and goes out through door.

Summing up
So, what are you left with at the end? First you have the whole scene played in wide angle, with everything contained in the one shot. Then you have a number of other shots from different angles of various sections of the scene. Because you have ensured that the action during every shot is as near as possible identical to the master wide angle, it will be possible to cut, say, from the master to the 2-s of Fred and Mabel at the sink, to the MCU of the taps, and so on at any one of a number of places. The cuts will then be determined in order that each piece of action may be seen in the final result from the most suitable angle in accordance with the dramatic interpretation of the script, and the resulting material available.

Medium close-up cupboard
(MCU cupboard)

Mid shot Mabel (MS Mabel)

Two shot at door (2-s at door)

67

Fred and Mabel: Edited Sequence

Finally, the scene has been edited, and the completed sequence might look like this:

Scene 1: Int. Kitchen. Day

1. W/A   MABEL IS PREPARING AN
2. MS Mabel   APPLE PIE/
3. W/A   FRED COMES IN/FROM THE GARDEN AND RUSHE
4. MCU tap   OVER TO THE SINK. HE TURNS/ON THE TAP
                    AND HOLDS HIS HAND UNDER THE STREAM OF WATE
5. 2-s at sink   MABEL GOES OVER TO HIM/

 MABEL: Fred, Fred, what's happened?
 MABEL EXAMINES HIS HAND

 MABEL: How on earth did you do that?

 FRED: The bloody adjuster stuck on the lawn mower.

 MABEL: You've got dirt in it.

 SHE PUTS HIS HAND BACK UNDER THE TAP

 MABEL: I'll get you a dressing

6. W/A   SHE/GOES TO THE CUPBOARD AND GETS
7. MCU cupboard   OUT/A TIN OF DRESSINGS

 MABEL: Do you want some antiseptic on it?

8. W/A   *FRED*: No, don't bother.
9. 2-s   MABEL TAKES A TOWEL AND GIVES IT TO FRED./
                    HE DRIES HIS HAND ON IT.

 FRED: Thanks love.

10. MCU dressing   MABEL STICKS DRESSING/ON FRED'S
11. Cu Fred   FINGER./HE WINCES

12. 2-s   *MABEL*: Did I hurt you?

 FRED: No. It's just a bit sore. (PAUSE)
 Right. I'll finish the lawn.

13. 2-s by door   BOTH GO/TO BACK DOOR

 FRED: What time's lunch?

 MABEL: Is half an hour all right?

 FRED: Fine. Give me a shout.

14. W/A   HE KISSES/HER AND GOES OUT.

68

THE EDITED SEQUENCE

1. Wide angle
2. Mid shot Mabel
3. Wide angle
4. Medium close-up tap and hand
5. Tight two shot
6. Wide angle
7. Medium close-up cupboard
8. Wide angle
9. Tight two shot
10. Close-up plaster
11. Close-up Fred
12. Tight two shot
13. Two shot at door
14. Wide angle

Direct and Indirect Continuity

We have examined the relationship of action, dialogue, props and costume within a scene. Now that scene must be related to others. Two forms of continuity are involved here: direct and indirect continuity.

Direct continuity

Direct continuity means that actions are carried over from one scene to the next with no time lapse. Reverting to the Fred and Mabel scene, there was direct continuity between the end of Scene 1, with Fred walking out of the back door, dressing on his finger, and the start of Scene 2, with Fred coming through the door into the garden, dressing still on his finger. What is important to remember is that these scenes will not be shot consecutively—indeed Scene 2 may well be shot first, therefore accurate notes on the beginnings and endings of scenes are vital.

Indirect continuity

Indirect continuity refers to continuity links between scenes that are not consecutive. It means that there is some sort of break—a time lapse, a scene interposed which deals with other characters or some other aspect of the story, but where there are continuity links between these scenes however spaced out in the story order. These different continuity threads might not be immediately apparent on reading the script or when each individual scene is shot, maybe days or weeks apart.

For example: Scene 1 ends with a man stuffing a package into the right hand pocket of his coat. Scenes 2 and 3 are centred round another character. Scene 4 shows our man from Scene 1 walking along a street to a rendezvous. It must be remembered that he is wearing a coat from Scene 1. Scene 5 shows the man meeting his contact. The man hands over the package. There is therefore indirect continuity with Scene 1, the package in the right hand coat pocket; with Scene 4, wearing the coat; and possibly for the contact with later scenes.

Remember that none of the above are shot in story order, which makes the whole matter more complex.

Knowing the script thoroughly prevents you from being caught unawares by indirect continuity.

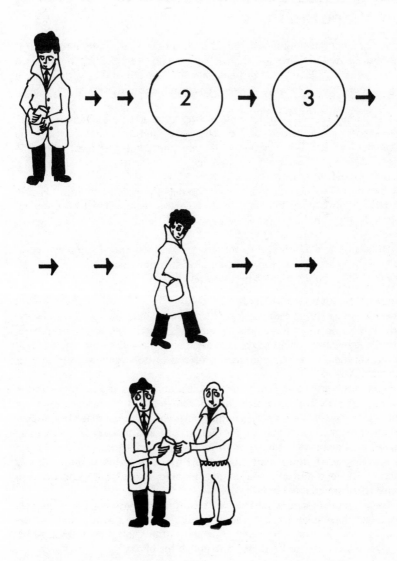

SCENES RELATED TO OTHERS

Scene 1 ends with the man putting the parcel into his coat pocket
Scenes 2 and 3 are concerned with other things
Scene 4 shows our man from Scene 1 (therefore there is indirect continuity from 1 to 4)
Scene 5 shows the man handing parcel over (therefore there is indirect continuity with Scene 1 and direct continuity from Scene 4)

Using Film Techniques While Recording on Videotape

A fairly recent development in television has been that inserts into electronic studio productions, are increasingly being recorded by lightweight video camera units, instead of being filmed. Sometimes whole dramas are even recorded in this way, where a few years ago they would have been filmed.

Very often, especially if the director is more used to the medium of film, the scenes are recorded out of sequence and the shots within the sequence are not taken together. If only one camera is used, then the scene is recorded using film techniques.

Problems of continuity

Recording in this way instantly raises the need for continuity and this can, and has, presented a dilemma for the person responsible for continuity when filming and also for shot calling, VT logging and timing when involved in electronic productions.

Does that person remain in the control room during recording, or go out on the set doing the job of continuity? It is not possible to do both, as the job of continuity cannot be done while peering at a screen.

How to resolve the problem

The simple answer is that you cannot resolve it, not entirely satisfactorily. Whichever you opt for, whether remaining on the set or in the control room, there will be times when you feel that you are in the wrong place. I think that the only sensible course to take is to do whatever your director wants.

If he is more used to film then he will probably want you to be on the set and possibly someone else can do your job in the control room. For remember that your job in the control room will have decreased in importance as there will probably be no shots to call and timings will be largely irrelevant, except, as in filming, to give a rough guide to the overall length of a scene. So the only remaining job to be done in the control room is that of VT logging, and you might be able to do that later using a non-broadcast quality copy.

But if your director is strictly an electronic television person, he will doubtless have planned the recording in a different way with, maybe shots to call, and he will probably remain in the control room himself or, at least expect you to be there to deputise for him.

Do you remain in the control room or go out on the set doing the job of continuity? Whichever you opt for, there will be times when you feel that you are in the wrong place.

How Do You Record What You See?

The continuity girl has a number of possible aids at her disposal for recording information.

I would not advise using a simple notebook or rough paper as there is quite a lot of varied information to be noted such as the footage and the time, and it is very easy to forget details.

You could have a portable typewriter on the set and type your notes during rehearsal directly on to the machine.

There are also printed continuity report sheets. These vary enormously in design and layout and in the amount of information they give. Two examples are shown here. Most report sheets are deficient in some aspect or other, and these deficiencies become apparent as soon as you start using them. But, despite the problems, it is preferable to use the correct forms as they require you to fill in the basic information you need.

You write on the sheets in rough and I file my own rough copy interleaved with the relevant page of script and carry it with me so that I can always refer to the shots when linking continuity with other senses.

Keep a copy of the script by you and write any dialogue changes as they occur, and also mark on the script any actions related to dialogue.

A Polaroid camera can be very useful for pictures of artists in their costumes or of sets, especially if they are complicated.

You might like to take pictures to establish artists' positions at the end of a master shot. But that can prove misleading later on if you have taken a picture at the end of Take 1, yet Take 4 is considered the best, and is the one to be used. The positions in Take 4 might be rather different.

The only trouble with using photographs is that everyone regards them for the absolute truth. Also, if the pictures are not really sharp because they are taken so hastily, even scribbled diagrams are more reliable.

TV FILM CONTINUITY NOTES

Date :

Title		Episode no. or title :				Slate no.	
Project no.							
Set-up / location		Int.	Day	Sync. Silent	Sequence no.		
		Ext.	Night	W/track W/t with camera	Shot no.		
		Script page no.		Shot list page no.			

Costume / make-up / prop notes

Roll no.										
circle TAKES printed	1	2	3	4	5	6	7	8	9	10
End board										
TIMING										
FOOTAGE										
REASON for use or n/g										

Action   Dialogue

Continuity Report Sheet: 1

Let us examine in detail what should be written on a continuity report sheet:

Production details
The first details to be written state the production number, title, date, director, cameraman and editor.

Slate number
Then comes the slate number. A slate number is the number given to each photographed shot. It is the means of cataloguing the shot. Almost always the first shot of the first day's shooting is called Slate No. 1 and proceeds consecutively until the last shot of the last day of shooting.

The slate number is shown marked up on a clapper board at the start of each shot. This board has a twofold purpose. In the days of silent pictures, each shot would be identified by the humblest member of the camera department holding up a piece of slate with a number chalked up on it. When talkies arrived, he would, in addition, bang together two pieces of wood—called a clapstick—to establish synchronisation between action and sound. Later the two were combined to form the clapperboard. The board is still called a 'slate' by tradition and the individual shot itself, being identified by a slate number is colloquially referred to as 'a slate'.

Scene or sequence number
Next mark down the scene or sequence number. A film script is divided up into scenes—each new location being a new scene. A scene is often called a sequence—but to be strictly accurate, a sequence is the final cut version of the scene. If there is a separate shot number, put that down.

Interior or exterior
Mark whether you are shooting an interior or an exterior scene, and if an exterior, note the weather. Just 'dull' or 'sunny' will suffice—the temperature will only be reflected in the faces of the actors who might be wearing light summer clothes on a brilliantly sunny but freezing day in February.

Day or night
Then record whether you are shooting a day or night scene. Also note whether you are shooting a dawn or dusk scene—you might be shooting a scene at dusk which is meant to represent dawn. It may look perfectly acceptable but it would not be self-evident to the editor unless he is informed of it.

TV FILM CONTINUITY NOTES   *Date:* 4 April 1974

Title THE CHANGES	Episode no. or title: 1	Slate no.
Project no. 3344/1051		68

Set-up / location				Sequence no. 7
KITCHEN	Int.	Day	Sync. / Silent	
Tracking 2-s Mrs Gore and Nicky	Ext.	Night	W/track / W/t with camera	Shot no.
	Script page no. 8		Shot list page no.	

Costume / make-up / prop notes

Nicky: school uniform (as photograph). Hair in bunches. Cardigan
done up. White socks and black shoes
Mrs G: Hair tied back. Plum cardigan thrown over shoulders -
brown/white smock under.

Roll no. 12	Sound roll 7									
circle **TAKES** printed	1	2	③	4	5	6	7	8	9	10
End board										
TIMING	1'23	20	1'15							
FOOTAGE										
REASON for use or n/g	NG action	NG camera								

Action	Dialogue
Starting on Mrs Gore's feet in rubbish. Plate of bread and butter in her right hand. Pours milk out of bottle into cup. Picks up cup and walks L to Nicky at table. Track with her. She puts plate down first then cup - in front Nicky. Sits on L Nicky. Nicky drinks. Nicky gets up facing mother and exits R - hold on Mrs Gore with her hands up to her face.	All scene

Continuity Report Sheet: 2

None of the information you have so far noted down should present any problems. Now you start on what is actually taking place at the location:

Location

You can if you want, write 'The Happy Haymaker's Pub, Grove Rd., Dorset', or you can just write 'pub'. It all depends on whether you have a separate list of locations on the schedule, or how important you feel the information to be.

Shot description

This should be written in the same box as 'Set-up/location' for quick, easy reference. If there is no such box, put it somewhere at the top of the page.

Sound

The next things to note down relate to sound. Is the shot taken sync—that is with camera and sound 'locked' together and running synchronously? Or is it to be a silent or 'mute' shot (with no sound recording being made)? If the sound is being recorded by itself without shooting a picture, this is known as a 'wild track', sometimes written as 'wildtrack'. The expression 'wild track with camera' refers to the sound being recorded simultaneously with the shooting of the picture but with no interlock between the camera and recorder. All under-cranked and over-cranked shots which have sound recorded for them at the same time must fall into this category.

One other term sometimes crops up—'guidetrack'. That indicates that the camera and sound are running in sync, the sound is intended only as a guide to the editor and is not of good enough quality to be used in the completed film.

Costume/make-up/props

The continuity report sheet must record details of costume, make-up and props.

At the start of a new scene always write what the artistes are wearing, how their hair is arranged and if their hairstyle is likely to change from scene to scene. Also make a note of any props they might be carrying, eg: a walking stick. Notes about make-up are only made for a major effect, like a cut cheek, which is supposed to heal up during the progress of the story. This would need to be checked to ensure that it is in the right condition for each stage of the story.

TV FILM CONTINUITY NOTES

Date: 4 April 1974

Title	THE CHANGES	Episode no. or title:		Slate no.
Project no.	3344/1051	1		69

Set-up / location		Int.	Day	Sync. / Silent	Sequence no. 7
KITCHEN					
CU Mrs Gore		Ext.	Night	W/track W/t with camera	Shot no.
		Script page no.		Shot list page no.	

Costume / make-up / prop notes

(as slate 68)

Roll no. 12	Sound roll 7									
circle TAKES printed	1	②	3	4	5	6	7	8	9	10
End board										
TIMING	40"	39"								
FOOTAGE										
REASON for use or n/g	NG fluff									

Action

Mrs Gore comes into shot as
she sits at table

Dialogue

from: (Mrs Gore sitting)
to: "...but you've got to
stay here"

79

Continuity Report Sheet: 3

Takes

A take is the recording on film of the action of a shot. If that action is not satisfactory for some reason, the same action is repeated using the same slate number, but marked on the clapperboard as 'Take 2'. If that is not satisfactory either, there is another take and so on until the director is satisfied. Say, for example, there are three takes on a particular shot. Take 1 is possible, Take 2 is unusable due to an actor forgetting his lines and Take 3 is good. The director might say that Takes 1 and 3 should be printed. Those numbers are circled in the camera report and the laboratories then only print Takes 1 and 3.

On your continuity sheet you should circle the accepted takes. The others are marked NG (No Good). But you should always give a reason *why* a take is NG. That is most important to the editor. For example, although everyone on the location might have decided that Take 7 was to be used, that take was damaged in processing. Therefore the editor must know if it is possible to use any of the other takes. Give as full a reason as possible. The take might have been good until right at the end when the noise of an aeroplane intruded. Write that down. The director might have been dissatisfied with an actor's performance or the camera operator dissatisfied with his framing. Write down the cause, whatever it is.

False starts

The director calls 'action' to start the shot but after a few seconds the actor might 'fluff' his lines. Instead of 'cutting' the camera and putting a new take number up, the director may tell the actor to start again, while the camera is still running. Make a note of that false start.

Timing and film footage

Give a timing for each take and the film footage indicated on the camera. Time from the moment the director says 'action' to when he says 'cut'.

Endboard

An endboard refers to the clapperboard. Sometimes the board is not put on the front of the shot but at the end, for example when something should be filmed instantly and without the delay of putting a board in front of the camera. The board is held upside down to indicate to the editor that it refers to the shot that has just ended.

Action and dialogue

The action is obviously what people do in a shot and the dialogue is what they say. I personally do not write all the dialogue out just the 'in' and 'out' cues. I mark any dialogue changes on the coverage script. I also type the dialogue in red to distinguish it from the action.

CONTINUITY REPORT SHEET: TAKES AND TIMINGS

TV FILM CONTINUITY NOTES *Date:* 4 April 1974

Title	THE CHANGES	Episode no. or title:	1	Slate no. 73
Project no.	3344/1051			

Set-up / location						Sequence no.
KITCHEN	(Int.)	(Day)	(Sync.) Silent	7
2-s			W/track	Shot no.
	Ext.	Night	W/t with camera	
	Script page no.		Shot list page no.	

Costume / make-up / prop notes

(as 68)

Roll no. 12/13   Sound roll 7

circle TAKES printed	1	Cam 13 (2)	3	4	5	6	7	8	9	10
End board										
TIMING	20"	25"								
FOOTAGE										
REASON for use or n/g	NG noise									

Action

Nicky standing centre.
Mrs Gore rises on L
- Nicky exits R

Dialogue

from: "Nicky you can't
       go to school"
to: end sequence

81

Information For the Editor

There are two ways of providing the editor with all the information he requires.

Typed-up continuity report sheets

You can type up all your rough notes on to a continuity report sheet and give it to the editor. That is the system most people follow and one which I used myself for many years until I happened to mention to my husband, who is a film editor, that all the additional typing in hotel bedrooms late at night or early in the morning were, for me, the one big drawback to the job.

His reply surprised me, for he said that he did not need half the information which had been so painstakingly given to him. For example, he was not interested in knowing what costumes the artistes wore— provided that continuity of costume was correct from shot to shot and scene to scene. Likewise the full description of the shot did not interest him. He did not need to be told that Jim entered shot frame L—walked R to the table—sat down—picked up the full glass of beer (with his right hand) etc. He had only to look at the relevant piece of film to find all that out!

So together we devised a far simpler way of providing the editor with the information he really does need called the continuity card system.

Continuity cards

The cards contain only the barest information about the shot, but it is information which the editor really needs. He needs to know which scene the shot relates to—he needs to know the slate number, the camera roll number and the sound roll number. Make a note if the take is sync or mute and use a separate card for wildtracks. Apart from that, he wants a brief description of the shot, e.g. W/A Henry's kitchen, and then, and vitally important to the editor, he needs to know about the takes: how many there were, which were NG and why, and which were acceptable. He needs nothing else *except* an accurate marked up coverage script to tell him what the shot covers in the scene.

The cards are simplicity itself. You will find that you have time during the day to write them out, reasonably clearly and legibly, and if you are working on a film series or filmed inserts for a series, I find that different coloured cards corresponding to the colours of the scripts are useful.

Having gone on at some length about the virtues of using cards, it is only fair to say that some editors do not like working with cards—they prefer pieces of paper which they can then place in a file. There is, of course, no reason why the basic information the editor needs should not be written on pieces of paper rather than cards. The important point is to give the editor the information he wants and not a lot of extraneous detail which he will never look at, but which has caused you hours of unnecessary work.

CONTINUITY SHEET FOR THE EDITOR

Title ....

....

Date ....

EPISODE	SCENE	SLATE

Camera roll*	Sound roll*	Circle whichever is appropriate:				
		SYNC	GUIDE	PLAY	MUTE	WILDTRACK
			TRACK	BACK		(to cover)

SHOT DESCRIPTION

* Could substitute boxes for 'Lens' and 'Focus' if more applicable.

Take*	Duration/ footage	Remarks (give full reason if take is NG)
	* circle accepted takes	
1		
2		

CONTINUITY CARD

Slate	Ep/Scene	Neg. roll	Tape roll

Description

Take	1	2	3	4	5
Duration					
Remarks					

Coverage Scripts

If you use the card system of continuity then it really is very important that you give the editor an accurate marked up coverage script together with the cards so that he can see what the shot covers in the scene.

Even if you do not use the card system, but type up continuity report sheets for the editor, he will find coverage scripts useful and you and the director might also find it helpful to have a marked-up script for yourselves.

On a copy of the script you make a separate line in a different colour for each shot, and write on that line which slate number it represents, together with a brief description. You will be able to find out the start and end of each shot by referring to your continuity notes. Do not put how many takes there were on each slate, just the number and description, eg Slate 342 W/A. If you do these accurately they will be a blessing to the editor and will also show you and the director at a glance the coverage of any scene.

Daily log

Purely for my own use as a form of cross-reference, I keep a log of what has been shot each day—the scene number, the slate number, the camera and roll numbers. This could be useful if you want to refer back quickly to a shot and only know that it was Slate 63 on Camera roll 10

EXAMPLE OF COVERAGE SCRIPT

SCENE 7 : GORE'S KITCHEN
         INT. DAY

68 Tracking 2-s

69 CU Mrs Gore
70 CU Nicky

72 MS Nicky → 2-s

THE ROOM IS NOW A SHAMBLES.
MRS GORE PRESENTS NICKY WITH
SOME BREAD AND BUTTER AND SOME
MILK. MRS GORE IS VERY DISHEVELLED
AND DISTRAIT. SHE LOOKS AS IF SHE
HASN'T SLEPT.

MRS GORE

That's all there is. We can't

cook anything now and even the

milk won't keep long now.

SHE GIVES AN UNHAPPY LOOK AT THE
FRIDGE WHICH IS STANDING WITH ITS
DOOR OPEN AND ITS SHELVES OUT.

NICKY

I'm now hungry anyway.

SHE DRINKS THE MILK

NICKY

I'd better go now.

MRS GORE

What?

SHE SUDDENLY TAKES IN THAT NICKY
IS DRESSED FOR SCHOOL.

MRS GORE

Nicky, you can't go to school.

Don't Forget The Boots . . .

Having gone into the theory of continuity on film drama at some length, I shall end this section on a more practical note.

It is Saturday and you are at home surrounded by continuity note books, pens, pencils etc. On Sunday afternoon you are taking a plane for a distant location, the first in the film you are working on. What do you take with you? I cannot give you any specific lists, but unless you are filming in a tropical country I strongly advise (at the risk of sounding like an over-protective mother) some thick sweaters, a windbreaker, a warm hat and scarf and . . . a stout pair of boots. Do not forget that while most of the rest of the unit can go off and warm themselves from time to time, if shooting is taking place, you are stuck there on the windy ridge, or in the damp forest or wherever, and if you are in the least prone to the cold, after a couple of hours standing you will feel frozen.

If you have ever secretly harboured the idea that filming is in any way 'glamorous' you can forget it. It has all kinds of attractions but there can be nothing less appealing than say, waddling out to a night shoot dressed in every available garment and hardly able to walk with the weight.

What else should you take with you for the job? Enough, but not too much of anything. That might sound contradictory, but the tendency is normally to take far too much of everything initially and then have the problem of transporting several large pieces of luggage from location to location. Of course the longer you are away the more you need to take, but it is generally possible to obtain further supplies—unless you are filming in a completely inaccessible spot.

On the other hand, do not forget to take small items essential for doing the job—pencil sharpeners, rubbers, a hole puncher and a selection of felt or fibre-tipped pens. You should of course, take plenty of continuity report sheets, spare scripts and filming schedules, as at least half the unit are likely to lose theirs.

DRESS FOR THE JOB

When packing to go away filming, make sure you take suitable clothes for the conditions you are likely to encounter. Be prepared for hours of standing in the coldest and wettest places.

The Realities of it all

Filming on location can be very tough. You will undoubtedly feel many times that there are easier ways of earning a living as you stand half-frozen and soaked to the skin in a field at three in the morning trying to film a group of sheep who refuse to cross the field from left to right. Or when you are lost in a mist on the hills with a director who has lost the map, lost his and everybody else's way, and even more important, lost the location caterers who are somewhere down in the valley.

Continuity itself is hard work. It requires an immense amount of concentration. Not only when shooting is actually taking place, but when nothing is apparently happening and most of the unit appear to be idling around. Most of them *are* idling around, but if the director and cameramen are working, then you must be working too.

Continuity also involves sitting up typing and marking up editing scripts often into the small hours while everyone else relaxes, enjoyably fraternising with the local populace.

If, however, you feel I have drawn too black a picture, do not forget that if you *do* prove to be one of those strange people like myself who love filming, and find continuity a most satisfying job, you will find like-minded people on every new film unit.

And the discomforts? . . . Well they do make for good after-dinner stories.

". . . you see, there I was, standing quietly watching the action, when I felt something tugging my hand. And it was this goat we'd borrowed from the local farmer to use as dressing. You know what it was up to? It was quietly eating my continuity notes in a contented sort of way . . ."

THE REALITIES OF FILMING

1. Filming can be frustrating—for example, filming sheep in the middle of the night
2. It can be annoying—when the director has lost the way
3. It can be hard work—typing at night when everyone else relaxes
4. But it does provide good after-dinner stories

The Work of a Production Secretary

The work of a production secretary in film is not as easy to define as the work of a continuity girl. The job can carry much responsibility for the organisation of the filming, or it can be a superior name for little more than a shorthand/typist.

In the BBC the two jobs of continuity and production secretary are rolled into one under the general title of "producer's assistant" (who is also involved in television studio work, a topic outside the scope of this book). Other companies and organisations arrange things differently.

I shall attempt, in the following sections, to give as complete a guide as possible to the work that takes place before and after filming. Some of the sections will, quite possibly, never be dealt with by a production secretary, or at least only indirectly, but the more that you know about the work involved before filming takes place, and after it is finished, the better.

THE PRODUCTION SECRETARY'S JOB

Your job as a production secretary can be interesting and rewarding. It can carry much of the responsibility for the organisation of the filming—or it can add up to little more than being a shorthand-typist or telephone minder.

The Script

Possibly the first job you have to do is to take a dog-eared, much scribbled over, almost indecipherable draft script, and turn it into a nicely turned-out, legible film script for everyone to use.

This might not be the final, definitive version, but everyone wants something to work from produced as quickly as possible.

There are many ways of laying out a script, but from much experimenting, I have devised my own method, described below.

Numbering
In filming everything is broken down into its smallest component—the script is broken down into scenes, which in turn, are broken down into shots—so it is important to number and label everything clearly.

At the top and bottom right-hand side of each page put the scene number and the page number, eg: Sc.11 (13). By putting the number on the bottom as well as the top it means that pages used in a clipboard can be identified, as the number will be obscured at the top.

If it is a television production and there are a number of episodes I have found a simple and useful method is to incorporate the episode number with the scene number, ie: Episode 2, Scene 1 would become 201, Episode 3, Scene 12 would become 312 etc. This means that there is never any confusion afterwards as to which episode a particular scene belongs.

Different colours
Always have each episode duplicated or photocopied on paper of a different colour, if possible. It makes things a little simpler to know that blue is Episode 1, pink is Episode 2 and so on. Always do everything you can to make things as simple and easy for yourself and everyone else, because when you are actually filming there is no time to sort out odd pages and work out where they belong.

Heading
Always begin a new scene on a new page. Type the scene number, location, interior or exterior and the time of day on the left-hand side of the page.

Body of script
Type the script on the right-hand side of the page leaving a very wide margin for notes etc. on the left. Type directions in capitals and the dialogue in lower case. Type dialogue in double space so that alterations can be made easily. Try not to carry over a piece of dialogue from one page to the next.

Sc. 506 (16)

SCENE 506 : EVANS KITCHEN. EARLY MORN.

                    MR EVANS IS SITTING STARING AT DEAD
                    FIRE, A POKER IN HIS HAND. HE LOOKS
                    TIRED. HE TURNS, STARTLED AS CARRIE
                    ENTERS. THEY STARE AT EACH OTHER.

                    MR EVANS

                    I was just coming to wake you.

                    CARRIE
                    Already?

                    MR EVANS

                    Your train goes at eight. It's

                    half past six now.

                    HE CROSSES TO WINDOW AND TAKES DOWN
                    BLACK-OUT.

                    CARRIE
                    Have you been up all night?

                    GRUNT FROM EVANS AS HE COMES BACK
                    AND BEGINS TO GET FIRE GOING

                    CARRIE
                    Auntie Lou?....

                    MR EVANS
                    Gone off with her fancy man. Did

                    you know?

                                        Sc. 506 (16)

93

Artistes and How to Book Them

You need to book artistes quickly as the whole process takes some time to complete.

Artistes
Artistes come in all shapes and sizes and to suit all requirements. They are found by the producer and/or director, who either have definite ideas of what they want, or sit closeted for hours with artiste directory and cast list laboriously trying to make a list of people to audition.

Agents
Artistes are looked after by agents, who find them work, look after their finances and generally administer to their needs. Some agents tend to specialise in actors with particular skills or abilities, others cater for all requirements. They can be pleasant and helpful or downright bloody-minded. They should be approached with caution.

Auditions
You might have to circulate the agencies, with details of the forthcoming production and a brief description of the cast needed. The agents then contact you with lists of people who they think suitable. After much discussion, you are given a shortlist of people to find out about. With this shortlist you ring the agencies and talk in deliberately vague and general terms in order to ascertain the availability of the person you are interested in for the dates necessary. Do not be specific because a verbal contract can be legally binding even if given over the telephone and without witnesses.

Auditions then take place with the selected people at a time and place previously arranged. After many such auditions, much discussion and countless references to the budget, a cast is agreed upon and con-tracts signed.

Names and addresses
As soon as the principal artistes are booked, get their names, addresses and phone numbers without delay and circulate them to people like the costume designer and make-up, who need to contact them.

Scripts and schedules
Let your artistes have scripts and schedules of filming in good time— always supposing they are ready in good time.

Hours of work
When you are actually filming, keep a note of the hours the artistes work and their travel time to and from the locations, as they may be entitled to payment for working overtime.

ARTISTES AND THEIR AGENTS

Artistes come in all shapes . . . and sizes. They are looked after by agents.

Extras and Walk-ons

The distinction between walk-ons and extras is often very fine, but very important to the individuals concerned and has a bearing on the fees paid.

Definition of an extra
An extra is someone who, in conjunction with others, is given general directions, eg: 'mill about' or 'act angry', but no individual direction and has no set words. A crowd of fans at a football match might all be extras. They might applaud and cheer as the mood takes them, but they are not instructed beforehand on what to say and do not perform any specific pre-arranged actions on cue.

Definition of a Walk-on 1
Out of our football crowd one person might be singled out to wave a flag on cue. He will then be a Walk-on 1. So would the policeman who points a warning finger at the flag waver.

Definition of a Walk-on 2
If the policeman were given some unimportant, unscripted words to say, he would then become a Walk-On 2. So would the flag-waver, if he was told to utter some appropriate epithets at the policeman. If, of course, the words are scripted, then the Walk-On 2 becomes an Artiste and is paid accordingly.

Where to obtain extras and walk-ons
Extras and walk-ons are employed by agencies and can be ordered in bulk. You can ask for 50 peasants, assorted, 20 female, 30 male, between the ages of 25 and 50, or be more specific in your requirements.

There are agencies that specialise in certain types, for example, there is one which caters for stunt men, heavies and fall guys in general, and will produce a fine range of villainous-looking characters at a moment's notice.

Don't get carried away
It can be a fairly heady business, ordering vast quantities of people, and one must be careful not to get carried away by the experience, and over-order. You must also be careful not to make mistakes because although extras are not costly individually, *en masse* the price can be formidable, especially if overtime work is incurred.

Suitable transport must be arranged and clear instructions on rendez-vous points given. It is usually necessary for them to be 'chaperoned' constantly, and usually someone is detailed to keep an eye on them and have them at the right place at the right time.

Always check and double check where extras are concerned. It is so easy to lose the odd one or two.

1. An *EXTRA* is a human prop

2. If an extra performs an action
   he becomes a *WALK ON 1*

3. If, in addition, he says a few
   unscripted words he then
   becomes a *WALK ON 2*

Children and Animals: 1

If at all possible, avoid children and animals. They are complicated to book, have an enormous number of rules and restrictions attached to their use and need a lot of looking after—even though they come with a retinue of chaperones, tutors, trainers and handlers. Often their minders can prove more of a problem to organize than they are.

Children and animals can waste an immense amount of time during filming. On balance, I prefer children because at least (if they are old enough) they understand what you are saying—but trying to make an animal do something on cue requires superhuman effort and patience— and a flexible shooting schedule.

Children on the other hand, although they understand, rarely give any indication that they have. They also have an alarming tendency to develop (in all ways) very rapidly during a film and the baby-faced child star whom everyone wanted to mother in the first week becomes the well-developed, sexy young lady whom everyone has quite different plans for, before many weeks have passed.

Where to find children
Children come from two sources, stage schools and non-stage schools. Much can be said for and against both.

Some directors never seek children at stage schools, preferring to make the rounds of ordinary schools and engage the help of drama organisers. Others cast solely from stage schools as they feel that the children will have a certain knowledge and discipline of the business to start with.

Wherever they come from, in the UK if they are under 16 they need licences from the local education authorities before they can appear in films.

Licences
Before the licences are granted, the authorities have to ensure that the *Children (Performances) Regulations 1968* will not be contravened. An application form for a licence has to be filled in and submitted, and this form goes into searching detail about every aspect of the filming.

CHILDREN AND ANIMALS

Children and animals can both be difficult to work with. Both need more time than the usual filming schedule can allow and vast amounts of patience.

Children and Animals: 2

Regulations

The regulations governing the use of children are very stringent, and should be examined in some detail before any individuals are booked and the filming schedule arranged. Children's hours of work, tuition, rest periods etc. are all laid down quite categorically and must be adhered to.

When filming, their hours must be carefully noted down as these details may be subject to inspection by the Education Authority.

Chaperones and tutors

Children under 16 need chaperones. These august ladies are to be found on any set sitting in a corner, knitting and discussing in depth how this production compares with the last, and exchanging the latest piece of gossip. They are in overall charge of the children. They must collect them from their home or their school, travel with them, keep an eye on them when filming and make sure that they are not getting overtired or being worked for too long without a rest. They are very important to the children as they are not connected with the production and there-fore acting solely in the child's interest. They must also take them home, or be responsible for them in the evenings if away from home.

If the filming occurs during school term time, tutors must be engaged to give a specified number of hours schooling each day.

Animals

Animals can be obtained from a number of places. There are a few agencies which deal in them, otherwise zoos, circuses and nature reserves are all possible places to search for the animal required.

They almost always come accompanied by a trainer or handler. The problems with animals start with their first day's shooting. They do not present any of the problems with regulations one encounters with children.

The provider of performing animals in the UK has to comply with the *Performing Animals (Regulation) Act of 1925* in regard to training the animals.

Officers from the local authority have the right to inspect the premises with the object of preventing cruelty to animals.

100

1

2

REGULATIONS FOR EMPLOYING CHILDREN AND ANIMALS

There are numerous regulations governing the employment of children and animals. They should be studied well. Any person under the age of 16 is classed as a child and is subject to these regulations. All children must be provided with qualified chaperones. All animals must be attended by their handler or trainer.

Location Filming: 1

As a production secretary, you probably do not have much, if anything, to do with finding locations, but once they have been found, it devolves on you to tie up the 'loose ends'—to get agreements in writing and arrange indemnity against heavy-handed film crews damaging the surroundings in which they work.

How to find your location
It is interesting however, to know how film locations are found, and why you ended up for ten weeks at a rural location with an unpronounceable name which is not shown on any ordinary map.

What to look for
1. *The script*. The script is obviously the first pointer. If the story is set in one of the hotter, dustier regions of Spain, it is no good trying to shoot it just outside London. You might well find a dusty region there, but what about the weather?

2. *Accessibility*. It is possible to take a film unit anywhere (almost). What must be considered is whether the cost and difficulties of travel to remote regions are worth while for guaranteed quiet, good weather and no one officiously demanding a permit.

A film unit, complete with artistes, make-up, wardrobe, props, lighting, camera crew, etc., is a very large, cumbersome body to move around. There is usually some very heavy equipment, large vehicles and a large number of people.

3. *Communications*. This leads off from the last point. It is necessary to have fairly fast, reliable communications with civilisation, and there must either be a means of transport available or special transport provided often at great expense.

4. *Facilities*. You may get all the peace and quiet needed in Outer Mongolia, but what about the hotels, the lack of electricity, or even the availability of public conveniences? This is to say nothing of evening entertainment; although a good film unit will always provide its own in one way or another.

HUNTING FOR LOCATIONS

Many things must be taken into consideration when looking for locations—not
just peace and quiet. Reasonable accessibility to civilisation is one factor as
a film unit is usually quite a large cumbersome body to move around.

103

Location Filming: 2

5. *Weather.* This is a difficulty that haunts many location-hunters in this and some other countries. Sometimes, time wasted in waiting for the weather to settle could have been better spent in transporting everyone to a warmer climate. In most cases, it is not important to have particularly good weather. But it should be consistent in scenes that are to be intercut.

6. *Noise.* This can be another problem. These days you have to travel further and further away from population centres to obtain real silence, and then you face other problems. It is amazing how noisy the heart of the country is, what with birds, insects, tractors, animals and so on, even when you think it is quiet.

7. *Friendliness of the locals.* You may have found the ideal spot—it is reasonably quiet, the weather is very good, the scenery just right and there are hotels just up the road . . . but when you arrive, you are met by an assortment of hostile people, brandishing umbrellas, rolling pins or other weapons, demanding:

(a) that you leave immediately,
(b) that you agree to pay large sums of money as 'protection'.
(c) that the crowd are all given parts—speaking ones of course.

If you were finding locations, those are the sort of problems you might encounter.

Studio filming
Film studios, by comparison, are a haven of rest. Everything is there to hand. But more and more films—at least the exterior scenes—are being shot on location and the luxury of the studio sets is not to be taken for granted.

1. Weather is an important factor. A run of bad weather can prolong a filming schedule alarmingly.

2. Noise is another problem to be aware of if you are shooting sync sound.

3. Friendliness of the locals—it helps ease the strain.

Accommodation

Booking suitable accommodation is often a very complicated business. It is essential to take time and trouble over it and to check and recheck the situation constantly.

It is better to overbook, initially, rather than omit to make bookings for people, as no-one would take kindly to your muttered 'I'm sorry, I forgot', if they have no bed for the night. But do not forget to cancel the rooms not needed, otherwise there will be an unnecessarily heavy charge.

Finding what is available
Get as much information as you can about the available accommodation in the area where you will be filming. Check whether you have to contend with the holiday season, the local carnival or the annual pole vaulting contest. If there is likely to be a shortage, make a block booking quickly and sort out the details later.

Finding the hotels
It is often not easy to find hotels close enough to the location that are satisfactory for price and number and size of rooms, and that can also meet all the varied requirements of such a varied group of people.

Making the booking
If it is a large booking, or made for a long period, many hotels come to some arrangement over a reduction in price.

Find out who wants what—for example, single rooms, single rooms with bathroom, double rooms etc. and try to arrange for these preferences to be upheld. It is not always possible, but if everyone is happy in their accommodation, it makes a lot of difference to the spirits and morale of the whole unit.

Some of the unit may well prefer to make their own arrangements. So long as this is acceptable to the director, they should not be forced to accept the booking you have made for them just because it simplifies things for you.

Your own booking
Make sure that you have adequate room to spread yourself and your mini office out sufficiently, and, if you are likely to be knee-deep in mud all day, you might prefer your own bathroom as well.

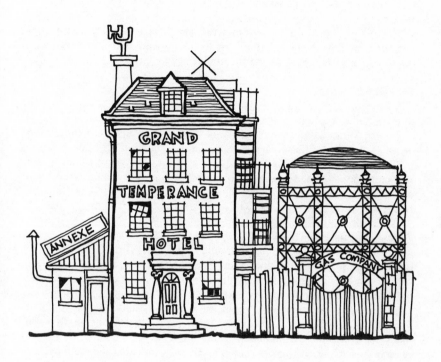

WHERE TO SLEEP EVERYONE

Trying to find accommodation to suit everyone can be difficult. Apart from
the practicalities of booking enough beds on the requisite nights in reasonable
hotels you always get problems with some members of the unit who will never
be satisfied with your arrangements.

Travel

It is very difficult to give specific details of what transport you will need and when. It depends so much on where your locations are, how many people prefer to make their own arrangements for travel and so on.

All you can really do is ensure that every single person on the unit has some means of travelling to the location—and that you have adequate transport actually on the location.

Travelling abroad

If filming abroad, make sure all travel arrangements are made in good time, as air and shipping lines tend to get booked up quickly.

Do not forget to make arrangements for travel to and from the airport or port—coaches, buses, vans, cars, taxis etc. must all be booked.

Check up on everybody's passport, and arrange visas if necessary. If vaccinations or inoculations are needed, find out what is required and make arrangements for everyone. Adequate amounts—and a good bit over—of foreign currency will be needed.

Travel in this country

Make sure there is more than adequate transport. If 15 people are to be collected from Point A and taken to Point B, book something slightly larger than a 15 seater coach as there may always be one or two extra people who turn up at the last moment.

In arranging transport you often have to hire all kinds of vehicles, fix rail tickets, and most important, give clear rendezvous points and times for transport and people.

Find out the local taxi or car hire firm in the area where you are filming and keep a note of their phone number.

Car parking

Make sure that there is a car parking space available at the hotel and at the location—or find out where vehicles can be left, not too far from the location.

TRANSPORT

Arrange suitable transport for everyone whatever the location, or make sure they have equally suitable means of their own.

Food (or to location cater or not . . .)

After accommodation and travel, food is one of the priorities. A number of firms specialise in feeding hungry film units, from around 20 to un-limited numbers of people.

They operate from anything, from converted buses, converted coaches and old lorries to the latest streamlined, fully equipped modern kitchen-on-wheels.

I cannot answer for all of them, but the ones I have experienced have all provided an excellent service—often rather too good in respect of one's waistline.

They are not cheap, but they do provide coffee and hot snacks in the morning, a full hot lunch and tea and cakes and biscuits in the afternoon. And the time saved in having hot food ready to hand, rather than hunting round pubs and cafes, is well worth it. The only thing they do not provide is a suitable place for consuming the food and the spectacle of members of a film unit trying to shield their steaming plates from the elements—usually rain—while making a dash from the caterers' van to the nearest cover must have amused many a local inhabi-tant.

Other types of catering

If location catering is not to be provided, then find out in advance what restaurants and cafes are in the vicinity. See whether any of them could cater for the numbers and type of meal you require and make advance arrangements with them.

Do not forget that while *your* lunchtime meal may consist of a piece of crispbread and some cheese, many people on the unit demand some-thing far more substantial, especially after a long, cold morning filming in the open.

Other meal breaks

If your filming schedule covers other meals, ie: breakfast or dinner, make similar arrangements with a local restaurant. If you have no caterers with you, arrange to take flasks of coffee and tea for mid-morning and afternoon, and do not forget the paper cups, spoons and sugar.

If you are far from civilisation

There may be times when you find yourself filming in remote areas with no food available from any source. There is only one answer and that is to carry your own packed lunch. This is not popular with film units and if you are forced to provide sandwiches made the night before by your hotel, for consumption by a hungry crew, do at least take flasks of hot soup and coffee with you.

LOCATION CATERING

Location caterers operate in a variety of vehicles and produce nourishing meals. They are usually very good value for the price.

The difficulty comes in trying to eat this tasty food while perched on the bonnet of a car doubled up to keep the rain from reducing your food to a sodden mess.

Breakdown of Scenes

After the script has been typed out, it is a good idea to type a breakdown of the scenes for use by various people. Such a breakdown will help in working out the schedule of filming, and be useful to the designer, the costume and make-up supervisors, the property manager and many others, as it is a quick and easy guide to each scene.

Scene No. & Page No.
Obviously you must give the scene number and the relevant page number of the script.

Location
Give the location; for instance, either 'garage' or the actual address of where it is to be filmed, if that is known.

Int/Ext: Day/Night
Is it an interior or exterior scene? Also, what time of day is it meant to be?

Scene type
I think it helpful to give a very very brief synopsis of the scene, which enables people to work from the breakdown without having to constantly refer back to the script.

Cast
List all the cast needed for the scene, even details of extras or walk-ons, and animals.

Props or notes
A space for a prop list or notes is a good idea if there is room.

EXAMPLE OF SCENE BREAKDOWN

"STRIKER" : EPISODE 3 : BREAKDOWN OF SCENES

Scene No.	Page No.	Location	Int/Ext Time	Scene type	Characters	Notes
301	2	Garage	Ext. Day	Mr Dyker angry with Ben	Mark Nick Ben Mr D Extras	
302	5	Office	Int. Day	Mr Robson on phone	Mr Robson	
303	6	Soggy's garden	Ext. Day	Dialogue while hanging out shirts	Soggy Jacky	
304	12	Caravan	Ext. Eve.	Sitting waiting	Mark Nick Soggy Bomber Wayne	
305	13	Caravan	Int. Eve.	Meal	Mr Dyker Ben	
306	15	Caravan	Ext. Eve.	Jacky arrives	Jacky Mark Nick Soggy	

Costume and Make-up

While things are daily getting busier in the production office, others are working equally hard in their own fields.

Costume

The first thing the costume designer does is to read the scripts and make notes on the period and the type of costumes needed. If it is to be a period production, much research will follow to ensure historical accuracy down to the smallest detail.

Consultations follow with the director over the designer's ideas, and agreement reached.

The designer notes the continuity of dress from one scene to another in the script and a careful watch is kept on this during the filming.

As soon as the artistes are booked, they are contacted, and measurements taken and discussions held with them. They often have to attend a number of fittings as the work of making costumes progresses.

Moving all the costumes around is a sizeable operation. Often filming on location can mean cramped, inadequate room for storage, washing, ironing and changing.

As with most things, speed is essential, and it is quite a feat to have a couple of coachloads of extras changed and on the set in double quick time.

Make-Up

The make-up artist also reads through the script carefully to determine the period and type of make-up needed. Research is done and notes made on any special make-up, like beards, wigs etc. and any peculiarities related to continuity, for example, a wound that gradually heals over a number of scenes.

The artistes are contacted in the same way as for costume.

During filming the make-up assistants constantly hover round the set ready to touch up make-up that is wilting under the lights.

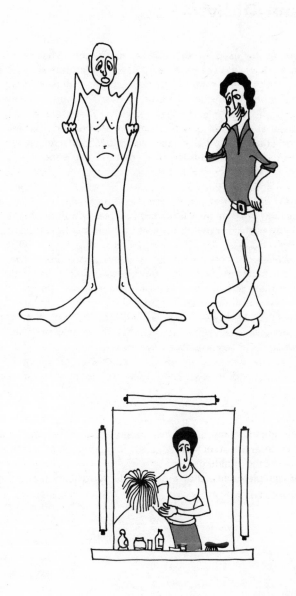

COSTUME AND MAKE-UP

Costume have their own problems contending with unusual shaped garments and unusual shaped actors, while make-up orders wigs, and researches into the correct make-up for the period.

Props and Design

Props that are to be used in the action, ie: a chair that is lifted in a threatening way or a book that is picked up and read, are called 'action props'. These are organised by the appropriate person, who might be the second or third assistant director, or the assistant floor manager in the BBC.

Other props that are not directly used in the action but are there merely as set decoration are called 'dressing props' and are the responsibility of the art director or designer, as part of the general design of his set.

Action props

The person dealing with them will have gone carefully through the script and the breakdown, marking all the props that are mentioned, ie: 'JOHN PICKS UP THE BOTTLE OF INK AND THROWS IT ACROSS THE ROOM'. He works out the continuity of such props from one scene to another, ie: in the scene following the ink throwing, there is no great time lapse, and there should be a large ink stain on the floor.

He also works out props that are not specifically mentioned in the script, ie: 'MARY IS MAKING A LARGE APPLE PIE'. For that he needs to get all the utensils and ingredients to make the action possible. There must be sufficient supplies to cover any retakes.

He works closely with the art director as the props needed in the action must correspond in style and type to the general dressing of the set.

Design

Much research goes into the period and mood of a production, especially when shooting interiors, whether specially constructed at a studio, or adapted from existing buildings.

Exteriors are simpler unless they are specially constructed streets, house fronts and so on.

116

DESIGN AND PROPS

This set shows the integral part design and props play in the director's overall
concept of the film. A great deal of creative effort and research has gone into
the design and construction of it.

Filming Schedule: 1

The high point of the work of a production secretary is the preparation and assistance in compiling the filming schedule. This schedule is the consummation of all the pre-filming work.

It will comprise all the different pieces of information gathered over the weeks regarding every single aspect of the filming, as well as the day to day schedule of filming.

It is a very important compilation, which is sent to everyone associated in any way with the filming.

Front page
The front page should give the details of the production, the name, the job number, the filming dates, and also the names and phone numbers of all the film unit and everyone connected with the film in a technical way.

Details of the laboratories—together with their addresses and telephone numbers—is also useful.

Cast list
Give an accurate cast list, with the names of all the artistes and extras. You might also like to give their agents' telephone numbers on this page. Do not give the private phone numbers of the artistes, as the schedule will be widely distributed and the artistes might be undesirably harassed if the numbers were too generally known.

Travel
Give detailed information on the travel arrangements that have been made including the times and places transport departs for the location, and lists of the people to travel at that time.

If there is a train service, copy out a train timetable from the principal towns to the location.

For those using their own transport and for guidance to the camera crews it might prove useful to include maps with the schedule, or at least explicit instructions on how to get there.

Accommodation
Give a full accommodation list, with the hotels' addresses, telephone numbers and prices of the rooms.

Location and contacts
List all the locations, their addresses and people to contact in connection with them. Also some useful addresses and phone numbers would include the local hospital, doctor, hire car or taxi service and police station.

118

Project Number: 2266/1003

"TIGER IN MY SOUP"

FILMING SCHEDULE
2 July-9 August 1975

PRODUCER	....	Jonathan Whitehead
DIRECTOR	....	Andrew Shelton
PRODUCTION ASSISTANT	....	James Delton
ASSISTANT FLOOR MANAGER	....	June Lammerton
PRODUCER'S ASSISTANT	....	Christine Turnham
DESIGNER	....	Leslie Johnson
COSTUME DESIGNER	....	Peter Huntley-Smith
DESIGN ASSISTANT	....	Joanna Wright
DRESSERS	....	Sally Downer/Ted Smythe
MAKE-UP SUPERVISOR	....	Suzie Cox
MAKE-UP ASSISTANT	....	Jane Lowton
PROPS BUYER	....	Ted Barclay
FILM OPERATIONS MANAGER	....	Jack Selby
LIGHTING CAMERAMAN	....	Frederick Selby
CAMERA ASSISTANT	....	Tony Shiner
GRIPS	....	Geoffrey Morgan
ELECTRICIAN (GAFFER)	....	Stan Wolfe
SOUND RECORDIST	....	Graham Ash
SOUND ASSISTANT	....	Hugh Barber
FILM EDITOR	....	Nicholas Johnson

Filming Schedule: 2

The way you set out the details of what scenes are to be shot each day is very much a matter of individual preference—yours and the production manager's.

A day to a page
It is sometimes thought simpler to type each day's details on a separate page, which can then be discarded when it is completed.

A week to a page
Others believe that the least amount of paperwork the better, and that it is far clearer to give all the information on as few pages as possible.
  Whatever format you favour, there are certain things you must write down:

Rendezvous
Clear instructions on the rendezvous time and place. I have stressed in earlier sections how important this is, as most problems can be sorted out, provided everyone meets up at the beginning.

Shooting order
The shooting order will have been worked out on the basis of the speed of shooting, availability of artistes and locations, making the best possible use of the time available.
  This shooting order commences with the date on which you are shooting, the scene or scenes you are shooting and then all the relevant details pertaining to those scenes, ie: the location, the characters involved in the scene, the time of day of the scene, and whether it is an interior or an exterior. You might also like to put details of the action props to be used.

Rescheduling
While the filming schedule should be as full a document as possible, changes may become necessary some time during the course of the filming. You might be held up by the weather, or unforeseen circumstances may force you to make alterations. You might even reach the stage where a complete re-scheduling is unavoidable. If that happens, do check up that any necessary alterations to hotel bookings, transport etc. are made.
  The really important thing about pre-filming work is that you should plan for possible contingencies, but if the 'impossible' happens, you should be flexible enough to be able to change things drastically if need be.

120

- 45 -

0830   MINI-BUS DEPARTS HOTEL, PORTHCAWL

0900   UNIT CALL ON LOCATION

1230   LUNCH

1800   approx. WRAP

LOCATION   43 CHURCH ROAD, PONTYPRIDD, GLAMORGAN

CONTACT   Mr P. Jones (address above, no telephone)

EPISODE SCENE PAGE	LOCATION	CHARACTER	NOTES
412 (37)	Ext. Day. Hillside	Carrie Nick Auntie Lou Mr Evans	
305 (20)	Int. Night. Bedroom	Carrie Nick	
212 (33)	Int. Night. "	Carrie Nick	
209 (28)	Int. Night. "	Carrie Nick	

TECHNICAL REQUIREMENTS

Black drapes

2nd camera arriving in evening

WEEK 9
MONDAY 3 DECEMBER

What to Take Filming

As you look round your office with its well-stocked cupboards and shelves, it is very difficult to envisage exactly what you need to take with you on location, and the quantities required. Of course, very much depends on where you are going and for how long, but a selection of the following might be useful:

Scripts and schedules
Always take plenty of these as people are apt to leave them in the most extraordinary places.

Anything to do with the production
Any files specifically related to the production, eg: your programme file, address book and diary must be taken.

Stationery and forms
If you use any standard forms, for example to do with artistes' hours etc., take enough of them, and a small amount of general stationery—notepaper, carbon paper, envelopes and stamps.

Miscellaneous
Here is a list of easily forgotten odds and ends which you would regret leaving behind.

Typewriter, Clipboard, Hole puncher, Stapler & staples, Adhesive tape, Paper and bulldog clips, Pencils/ball pens, Pencil sharpener, Rubber, Ruler, Rubber bands, Spare files, Spare folders, Rough paper, String, Scissors.

In addition for continuity
If your job is combined with that of continuity girl, take in addition:

Continuity report forms
1 set of coverage scripts
1 set of rough continuity scripts
1 set of scripts (to be interleaved with continuity notes for your daily use)
Stopwatch
Polaroid camera and film

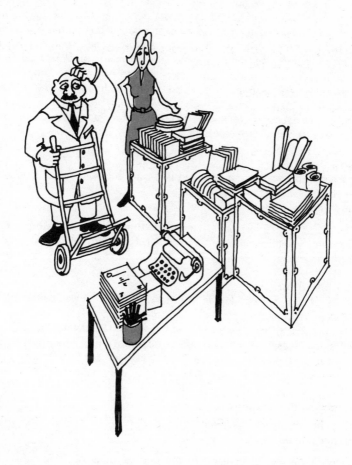

PACKING UP YOUR OFFICE

Do not take too much away with you. You only have the problem of transporting
it around from location to location and then probably taking most of it home
unused at the end. Work out a list of essentials beforehand and stick to it.

123

What Happens After a Day's Shooting?: 1

I am including this section purely because I used to be very puzzled when I saw camera and sound assistants departing at speed at the end of each day's filming to put the film and tapes on a train. I had no idea what happened to them afterwards, and between the actual filming and the film editor fulfilling his role, there was a blank in my mind filled only with the name of a mysterious place called 'The Labs'.

To avoid similar distress, I shall explain what happens after a day's shooting.

Firstly it is necessary to know that the picture and sound are dealt with as two separate processes.

Picture

The rolls of exposed film are sealed in film cans and sent to the laboratory processing the film for the production.

The principal laboratories in the UK are:

Technicolor, Rank Laboratories (Denham), Humphreys Laboratories, Kays Laboratories, Filmatic Laboratories, Reeds Laboratories, Universal Laboratories, Colour Film Services, Henderson Laboratories, Brent Laboratories.

At the laboratories

The cans of film are opened in the dark and the film threaded on to a processor. This machine runs the film through a processing bath appropriate to the type of film the cameraman has used (Eastmancolor negative, Ektachrome reversal, Black and white negative etc.). After processing, the negative, or master, is ready for subsequent printing. In the case of 35 mm the cameraman specifies whether each individual take is to be:

(a) printed in colour
(b) printed in black and white
(c) not printed at all.

Because of the risk of damage to the original, rolls of 16 mm film are not broken down (cut up) into individual slates (sections for each shot). The whole roll has to be printed either in black and white or colour. In the case of a roll of 16 mm film composed entirely of NG takes the cameraman could either specify the roll to be developed only, without printing, or more likely, throw it away.

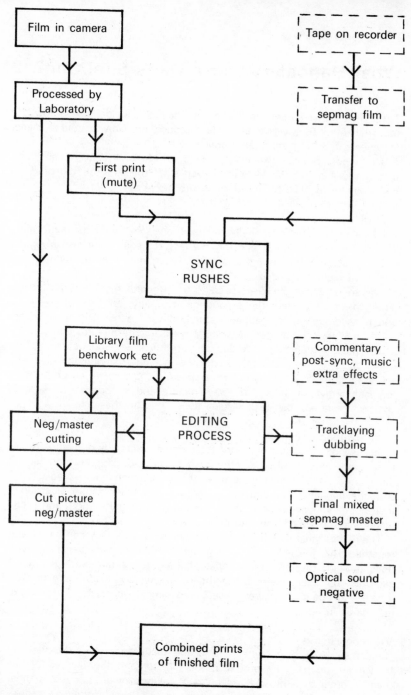

AFTER A DAY'S SHOOT—PICTURE

This is what happens to the film after a day's shooting.
In television, the show print is usually mute and is shown in conjunction with
the final sepmag track on a double-head machine.

What Happens After a Day's Shooting?: 2

These first prints known as 'rushes' in the UK and 'dailies' in the US, are viewed first by a viewer at the laboratories, probably at double speed. He checks for technical quality only.

This whole process can take place overnight in the major labs. and it is possible to have a technical report from the labs. on the previous day's filming by 8.30 in the morning the next day.

Sound

On location, sound is normally recorded on $\frac{1}{4}$ in. wide magnetic tape. The tape machine records not only the required sound but also a regular pulse of some form from the camera. These pulses correspond to the frames of picture exposed.

The sound tapes are dispatched to a re-recording, or transfer studio, either inside or outside the production company, and are played back and re-recorded on to magnetic sound film, of either 16mm or 35mm width, usually according to the gauge used for the picture.

The pulse which was recorded on location is fed into intricate electronic equipment which ensures that the machine carrying the magnetic sound film runs at precisely the same speed as the *camera* ran on location for each individual take. This way, picture and sound can be kept in step with one another, if they have been lined up that way.

Synchronising rushes

It still is not possible to put the first roll of sound and picture on to a projector and simply view the rushes with sound corresponding to the picture. This is mainly because the cameraman and recordist who shot the film and recorded the sound will not have started or stopped their equipment at precisely the same point. Also mute shots and wildtracks may be mixed with the other material.

The rushes must therefore be 'synchronised' before they can be viewed together. This job is normally done by the film editor's assistant, who goes through the rolls of material aligning the sound and picture of each take by means of the clapperboard. His work is made more difficult where end-boards have been used, and almost impossible if there are no boards at all.

Viewing rushes

Once they have been synchronised the rushes are ready for viewing by various people. The producer, the director and the film editor see them in order that the final selection of takes may be made, and other people, principally the cameraman, want to see them for their own interest.

After viewing, the editor breaks down the rolls of picture and sound and the editing process begins.

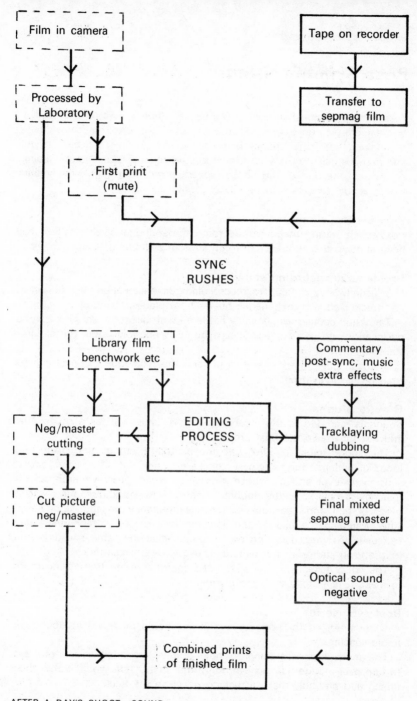

AFTER A DAY'S SHOOT—SOUND

This is what happens to the sound after a day's shooting.
In television, the show print is usually mute and is shown in conjunction with
the final sepmag track on a double-head machine.

Post Synchronising

After filming has finished and editing begun, there is little for the production secretary to do except tie up any loose ends left over from filming, ie: making sure any unpaid bills are settled, artistes are paid in full and perhaps helping draw up a final budget for the total cost of filming.

Towards the end of the editing schedule you might get involved in typing scripts for post-synchronising sessions.

Post synchronising
Post synchronising means re-recording the sound after the picture has been shot, in the controlled surroundings of a dubbing theatre.

Problems in recording sound
It is usually very difficult to record dialogue on location that is 'clean' and not mixed with extraneous noises from planes, traffic etc.

Television companies generally battle on with using the sound recorded on location and try to get as clean sound as possible under the circumstances.

In the feature film industry in general the technique of 'post-synchronising' is often used.

How it is done
Sound is recorded at the location but it is considered as a guide only and not for use in the final production.

This sound track, together with the picture, is cut up and made into loops of perhaps one or two sentences at a time.

The artiste or artistes whose words are being post synchronised on that day are called to the dubbing theatre. They are shown the relevant piece of film and hear their original performance on the guide loop. After watching the picture and listening to this loop a few times they can usually repeat their spoken performance at the same speed as the loop and in step with the picture. Those lines are recorded.

The editor takes the newly recorded sound away to the cutting room to make it fit exactly with the picture.

Post sync script
A script prepared for post synchronising should be typed in double or treble spacing.

The most important thing to note is that the artist does not have to turn over a page half-way through one 'loop'. This would throw their timing and probably make a rustling noise on the track.

THE DUBBING THEATRE

For post-synchronisation, the artist sits in a dubbing theatre and repeats his
dialogue in step with his performance on the screen.

Introduction to Documentary Filming

I have classified any filming that is not drama, as documentary.

Research

Research is the basis of preparation for much documentary filming and your taste for detective work will determine whether you enjoy being involved in documentaries.

The extent to which you are involved in the research depends on who you work for. If you are condemned to 'minding the phone' and typing the letters and given no scope in the preliminary research, you will understandably be bored and frustrated—unless you like phone-minding and letter typing as a full time occupation.

Learning about new things

The aspect I particularly like about the work is the amount you learn about subjects of which you were formerly ignorant. You might well have been ignorant of the subject as it never interested you. You might indeed view with extreme scepticism, as I did, the prospect of a few months research into the history of a famous football stadium, if, like me, you have always kept well clear of organised sport.

But by the end of the research period I was ready to admit that I had learned a good deal that was fascinating about the subject.

Additional work to research

Once the groundwork is done, you will be concerned with setting up the filming—booking film crews—working out the schedule etc.

Unlike drama, during documentary filming only a simple record of the shooting is necessary. There may, possibly, also be some elementary continuity work.

After filming, you may be involved with booking narrators, preparing commentary scripts, helping to find music, photographs, and archive film from film libraries.

But first comes the bread and butter of documentary work: research.

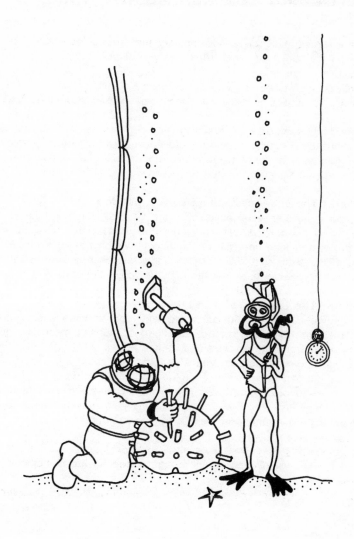

DOCUMENTARY FILMING

Research for documentary filming can give you an insight into subjects you might never otherwise explore.

'Find Out All You Can About . . .'

You have started work on a documentary film about '. . . .'. You have been given the above directive. Where do you begin?

The subject
Obviously the subject of the documentary will give you the first lead.

Example 1: The history of aviation
A film about the history of aviation could take you on a lengthy journey through libraries, film libraries, museums, the air forces of various countries, the historic societies devoted to preserving old planes, etc.

Example 2: The sun-worshippers of S.E. London
A film about the sun-worshippers of South East London will take you to South East London (probably at dawn) to witness the worshippers in action—to a second floor flat in Camberwell which houses the headquarters of the sect—to the libraries for some historical background and to the local newspaper who first brought the subject to light.

Example 3: The training of nurses
A film on the training of nurses would take you to various teaching hospitals, to the library for some background, to nursing manuals, and to much discussion with teachers and trainee nurses.

Once you know the subject, you can start researching into the most obvious aspect and other paths of exploration will open up.

The more you dig around, the more you uncover, and the amount of time, energy and patience you devote to the subject depends on the needs of the film and your instinct as a bloodhound.

Other bodies for research
Below is a short list of places which might prove helpful in beginning your research:

Libraries
Town halls
Local councils
Government departments
Law courts
Welfare institutions
Army/Navy/Air Forces
Universities
Polytechnics
Newspapers (national and local)

RESEARCH

Libraries can be useful starting points for research.

The past can often be found in film libraries.

Film Libraries

It is possible that the documentary you are involved with may include a certain amount of film that has already been shot, such as old newsreels.

This film is found in film libraries. These libraries hold all kinds of film, and tend to specialise in a particular type, eg: Pathé Film Library contains a large amount of old newsreel film, taken by Pathé News.

The amount of film you want could vary from a five second shot of an earthquake to a whole programme devoted to old newsreel and historic film. Whatever you want, you should be able to find a film library to help you.

The libraries charge a fee for use, the charge being determined by the amount of film footage you use in the final film, probably together with a search fee.

The film they hold takes various forms, and you should consult the film editor in order to determine exactly what form he wants ordered. This is particularly important when using black and white library film in a colour programme.

List of film libraries
Below is a list of the principal film libraries in the UK.

BBC Film Library (567 6655)
British Airways Film Library (202 5342 Ext. 2410)
British Transport Film Library (262 5242)
Central Office of Information (928 2345 Ext: 8074)
E.M.I. Film Library (953 1600)
Pathe Film Library (437 0444)
Film Centre Production Library (387 4052)
Granada Television Library (061 832 7211)
Imperial War Museum (735 8922)
INDEX Film Library (637 8741)
I.T.N. Film Library (637 2424)
National Coal Board Film Library (235 2020 Ext: 392)
National Film Archive (437 4355)
Slade Film History Register (387 5811)
Visnews (965 7733)

FILM LIBRARIES

Film libraries hold a wide variety of film and different libraries tend to specialise in certain subjects.

Graphics

Photographs
Research for photographs can be from books, newspapers, magazines and picture libraries. An important point to remember is that the so-called 'Academy' aperture or TV frame has an aspect ratio of 1.33 to 1 (4 across and 3 up). This means that if a photograph or illustration is to be filmed in its entirety, it must be in the ratio of 4:3. Very few photographs are in this format.

Therefore, when they come to be filmed, only a certain area of the photograph can be included in the frame. Filming of titles, photographs etc. is known as 'bench' or 'rostrum' filming and is normally undertaken by a specialist department or firm and is not normally done by the film cameraman. For example, you find an upright postcard size picture of the High Sheriff of Inverness in his official regalia. A static shot of this photograph can only include his head and shoulders, and to show the whole photograph in the film one must either pan from his feet to his head or vice versa.

Camera movement in bench filming can often be used from choice rather than necessity. Take, for example, an old school photograph of a class of 12 year olds, one of whom has just become a major public figure. The illustration is far more effective if one starts the shot with the whole area of the photograph and then zooms in to the relevant prodigy.

Titles
Graphics, titles and photographs specially taken for the production should be composed in the correct ratio. Title cards are normally 24 × 18 in or 12 × 9 in.

All bench work should generally be on the same film stock and in the same gauge (16mm, 35mm or whatever) as the rest of the production.

An exception is when titles are to be superimposed on a live action background. Here it is important to consult the film editor as to how he wants the art work shot.

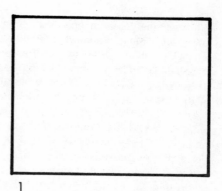

1. The Academy or TV frame.

1

2. A static bench shot of this photograph would only give a portion of the picture. Therefore you might need movement.

2

137

When Filming for Documentaries

When all the research and preliminary work is done and you get out and start filming, your work mainly consists of helping to make the whole operation run as smoothly as possible.

You may find yourself placating irate gentlemen, who are unable to park their cars in their usual spot due to all the crew vehicles. You might spend hours explaining to members of the public, who always seem to congregate at an alarming rate when filming is taking place, what it is you are filming. You will need a pocketful of small coins to bribe children to go away and you find yourself chatting away to nervous old ladies who have not had a wink of sleep the previous night, partly in dread of their forthcoming film interview, and partly for fear of dis-arranging their expensive hair-do, in a manner quite unlike your usual, rather reticent self.

In short, you are acting as trouble-shooter extraordinary, paver of ways and smoother out of difficulties.

Apart from the pocket full of coins you must take sufficient funds to cover the many expenses incurred when filming.

The best advice I can give is to be prepared for anything to happen, then you will not be put out.

TROUBLE-SHOOTER

Much of your job during actual filming will be that of general factotum, fixer and trouble-shooter. You will smooth the way for an untroubled, fast, efficient film shoot, and if anything goes wrong you will be blamed.

Shot Listing

Shot listing for documentary filming is much simpler than continuity in drama filming. You must keep an accurate daily record of the shooting, and there may be simple continuity involved. Of course it is not always easy to make this shot list when you are doing a hundred other things at the same time, and if you really cannot manage to shot list at the time of shooting, you should do it as soon as possible after filming, from the rushes.

When shot listing, you should note the following:

Slate number
Give slate and take numbers.

Shot description
It is not necessary to go into lengthy detail about the shot. Just the shot size, and what it consists of, is all that is necessary, eg: W/A River Thames from Strand-on-the-Green, Chiswick, panning from Kew Bridge, R-L.

Sound
Always write whether the shot is taken sync or mute, and make a note of any additional wildtracks.

Footage
Either time the shot with a stopwatch or make a note of the footage.

Interviews
At some stage or other you will almost certainly be shot-listing for an interview. There are one or two things to note about it.

Unless you are extraordinarily good at shorthand, or the interviewee speaks very slowly, you are unlikely to get it all down on paper. You can either take a tape or cassette recorder and make a rough recording which you can transcribe later, or it might be sufficient just to take note of the questions and the beginnings and ends of the answers.

The questions are important, as very often the interviewee is filmed first, then one or two 'noddies' as they are called are shot. These are shots of the interviewee, not talking, but listening. Then the camera might be turned round and the interviewer asking questions filmed, with a few 'noddies' of his at the end. It is important therefore that you know exactly what questions he asked. Finally, or at the beginning, a wide angle establishing shot is taken.

SHOT LIST   Page 10

Interview with James McDuff
Sec. of Laxford Bridge Steam Preservation Society

Interviewer: John Jenkins   Director: Peter Ladd

Slate	Description	Sync/Mute	Duration
32/1	MS James McDuff	Sync	2'04
	Q: Mr McDuff, you are Secretary of the Laxford Bridge Steam Preservation Society. How long has the Society been going?		
	A: Well, it was in 1956... ...running ever since.		
	Q: The railway operates in a very remote part of Scotland. How does it pay its way?		
	A: It doesn't...trips to the coast and such like.		
33/1	MS a/b	Sync	30" NG
	Q: Do you get many railway enthusiasts up here?		
	A: Well, there are many.. many..er..I'm sorry...		
33/2	Q: Do you get many railway enthusiasts up here?	Sync	1'10"
	A: Oh, we get a fair amount ...not encouraged.		
34/1	Q: One last question. How do you respond to the jibe about over-grown schoolboys playing with trains?	Sync	25"
	A: What's wrong with being an overgrown schoolboy?		
	Q: Thank you Mr McDuff.		
35/1	2-s Interviewer and Mr McDuff	Mute	35"
36/1	R/A MS Interviewer (all questions as above)	Sync	35"
37/1	Noddies interviewer	Mute	53"

Film Footage

Whenever I have mentioned film footage in this book I have been talking about 'real' feet. If, for example, a shot is 15 feet long, after processing you could measure it with a tape measure and find that it is 15 feet in length.

But when we get to the cutting room or the dubbing theatre we find that in the case of 16mm film, a foot appears to be 5 in long!

The reason is as follows: one real foot of 35mm film contains 16 frames of picture. One real foot of 16mm film contains 40 frames of picture. Since both gauges run at the same speed in terms of *frames* per second, not in terms of *length* per second, and the height of the 35mm frame is $2\frac{1}{2}$ times greater than that of the 16mm frame, a given length of 16mm film lasts for $2\frac{1}{2}$ times longer on the screen than the same length of 35mm film.

Footage counters

In the dubbing theatre or on the editing machine, a footage counter is provided. In practice, with 35mm film one digit represents one real foot of film, which lasts two-thirds of a second.

When the machine is running, the digits change every two-thirds of a second which is a convenient interval for cueing purposes, ie: commentary, spot effects etc.

The problem comes with 16mm film. The same arrangement, ie: counting real feet, would mean a digit change giving a cueing interval every $1\frac{1}{2}$ seconds, which is not very accurate. Thus, 16mm editing equipment and dubbing theatres very often have footage counters which register the length of the film which would be passing through them if that film were 35mm. Remembering that there are 16 frames of 35mm film to a real foot, the 16mm machine in fact registers units of 16 frames, lasting in time two-thirds of a second, as with the 35mm machine. If you measure 16 frames of 16mm film against a ruler, you will find it is just under 5 in long.

Timing and costing

As a general rule, for timing purposes with 16mm film after shooting, one talks in terms of 35mm feet, ie: a 10 min 40 sec film is 1,000 ft long. For costing purposes the same film is regarded as 400 ft.

The exception to the costing rule is when a 16mm production contains library film, the original of which is 35mm. In this case the "price per foot" applies to the 35mm footage, ie: $2\frac{1}{2}$ times the 16mm footage.

A footage conversion table is an essential for a production secretary working in documentaries, (see page 150). There is also a stopwatch on the market whose dial is marked in seconds, 16mm feet and 35mm feet.

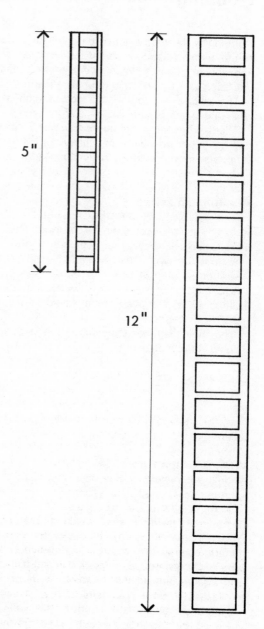

Both strips of film consist of 16 frames. The 35mm strip (on the right) is 12 inches long or one foot. But the 16mm strip (on the left) is only 5 inches long. Therefore with 16mm film a 'foot' appears to be only 5 inches long! Unless this is understood it can cause misunderstandings in the cutting room and dubbing theatre.

143

Dubbing

Dubbing is the term used to describe the process of mixing the various sound tracks (actuality sound, re-recorded sound, commentary, music and effects) together to form one master sound track for the film. This operation takes place in a dubbing theatre.

The picture is shown on a screen with a footage counter normally changing digits at intervals of $\frac{2}{3}$ of a second.

The first operation that might take place, either on the same or previous day, is to record the commentary. In order to write the commentary script you must previously have compiled a post-production pre-dubbing script.

Pre-dubbing script

This script is merely an accurate shot list of the edited film, with the footages given on one side. You make this shot list by working from a viewing machine that runs picture and sound and has a footage counter.

You should write the footage from the start and not the end of the first shot, ie: start at 00.

The director or script writer writes the commentary to your shot list. They can make a pretty accurate script by writing two words to one foot.

You may then be required to type a dubbing script for the person reading the commentary.

Dubbing script

You type the commentary only, in treble spacing and with the footages marked in the left-hand margin. Leave a big margin on the left for any notes or alterations, and never carry a sentence forward from one page to the next.

What you don't do

After the commentary has been recorded, the operation of mixing the various tracks together takes place.

There is little for you to do while this is going on. There is absolutely no point in taking a stop watch and attempting to get a timing for costing purposes, as (a) the stopwatch is not as accurate as the film footage counter, (b) you would drive yourself insane as the film keeps running backwards and forwards, and (c) you would drive everyone else insane, particularly the dubbing mixer, who might desperately try to erase the 'clicks' he hears until he realises that you are the guilty clicker, and that the fault is not on the sound tracks.

During the final run through when the master sound track is finally checked and usually a safety copy (which is a copy of the final mix master track) made, it is a good idea to note down the various footages as it saves you from viewing the print and doing the job later on.

144

PRE-DUBBING POST-PRODUCTION SCRIPT

Shot No.	Description	Footage
1	W/A harbour	000
2	LS boat about to dock	032
3	MS man walking down gangplank	041
	(steps on to land) S/I MAIN TITLE	047
4	Man walking on to railway platform	064
5	LS train coming into station	092
6	Train stops, man gets in	119
7	L/A train departing	143
8	Int. train. Man speaking SYNC	168
9	B/W Library shot. LMS steam train	182

COMMENTARY SCRIPT

Footage	Commentary
119	NARRATOR: I'm now going to travel on the wildest railway line in Great Britain, part of which was originally called the Duke of Sutherland's railway. When the line was built, it had a private station at Dunrobin to serve the Duke's castle. That station's still there.

(clear by 143 for train effects)

(168   SYNC TO CAM. IN TRAIN
There's even a buffet car on this
amazing service which runs three times
a day but never on Sundays. Before
the war they served kippers.)

Copyright: 1

Copyright is the protection the law (in the UK, the Copyright Act 1956) gives to a person or organisation for something that they have created.

Simple copyright
In its simplest form this could be a literary work, a painting, a photograph, a musical composition, a recorded musical performance. But such things as gramophone records, illustrated books and films involve multiple copyright.

Multiple copyright
A gramophone record of a copyright composition involves not only the composers' copyright, but that of the performers and the recording itself as well.

Protection
The protection the law gives ensures that no one other than the copyright owners have the right to use the work unless authorised by the owner who is thus able to charge a fee.

It is particularly important that permission is obtained before any material is used in a film, if that material is copyright.

Film
Copyright in a film belongs to the film maker. However it is not as simple as that, as the film distributor may have bought some or all of the rights in that film, eg: the film *Heavens Above* was a Boulting Brothers production, distributed to cinemas by British Lion Films and available on 16mm for non-theatrical use by the Rank Film Library. Before using an excerpt of this film in another production, one has to trace which organisation is in a position to give the necessary permission.

Copyright extends for 50 years from the film being registered under Part III of the Cinematographic Films Act of 1950 (UK), or, if not registrable, 50 years from when it was first published, ie: when copies were sold or hired to the public.

MUSIC COPYRIGHT

A commercial recording involves multiple copyright: The composers';
The performers'; The recording company's.

Copyright: 2

Photographs
Copyright extends for 50 years from when the photograph was first published.

Artistic works
Copyright extends for 50 years from the year of the author's death.

Music
The composers' copyright extends for 50 years from the death of the composer. But be careful, because if the work has since been re-arranged by someone, the arranger enjoys the same copyright protection as the original composer.

With gramophone records the copyright resides with the gramophone manufacturers for 50 years from when the recording was first published.

Literary works
Copyright extends for 50 years from the end of the year in which the author died.

One final word. If, say, an artist is commissioned to do a work, then the copyright of that work may well rest with the person or organisation who commissioned it and not with the artist.

NOTE: All references to copyright made here apply to the law in force in the UK, although *in general* they apply in the US also.

LITERARY WORKS

Copyright extends for fifty years after the death of the author.

Post Production Script

Throughout this book you have probably been aware that a large part of your job, as a production secretary or as a continuity girl, has been to record events. These are events that have not yet taken place, as with the filming schedule, events that are in the process of taking place, as with the continuity report sheet or the shot list, and events that have already taken place, as with the post production script.

This script is the written account of the film. It contains *everything* that is in the finished film, and more than that, it contains the source of everything you have used, whether it be specially shot for the production, film library material, music or photographs.

Use of the script
It has a twofold use:

1. For costing purposes. As it contains the original source of everything used in the film, including the artistes, and gives the copyright source, paying the right people is comparatively simple.

2. For posterity. If anyone in the future wishes to use any part of the film, it will be easy to find all the requisite information from the post production script.

What the script contains
Against the film footage, the script contains all the action (in the form of a shot list), together with the dialogue.

Library film
If library film is used, this is shown against the film footage, and the copyright source is given.

Music
Full details of all music must be given—whether it is from disc or specially recorded, and details of the maker, the performers, the composer and the record publisher given.

Photographs
The original source of all photographs must be given.

In addition to the above, which would be shown against the film footage, thereby giving the duration of all the individual components, the following details should appear:

The names of all *artistes* appearing in the production, or the *commentator* or *narrator*.

In the case of drama, the *author* and *dramatist*.

Anything else you can think of to make the lives of future generations of production secretaries a little easier.

Footage	Action	Sound
000	W/A harbour	Natural F/X and music "The Three Elizabeths" Suite Comp. & cond. Eric Coates Orchestra: The New Symphony DECCA LK 4056
032	LS boat about to dock	
041	MS man walking down gangplank	
047	Isteps on to land) S/I MAIN TITLE	
064	Man walking on to railway platform	Music ends 064 - train F/X only
092	LS train coming into station	
119	Train stops, man gets in	COMM: I'm now going to travel on the wildest railway line in Great Britain, part of which was originally called the Duke of Sutherland's railway. When the line was built it had a private station at Dunrobin to serve the Duke's castle. That station's still there.
143	L/A train departing	F/X train departing
168	Int. Train. Man speaking	SYNC DIALOGUE: There's even a buffet car on this amazing service which runs three times a day but never on Sundays. Before the war they served kippers.
182	B/W Library shot. LMS Steam train near Altnabreac (Private collection: R. McTavish, 4 Shaw St. Lochinver, Sutherland)	Music "The Four Centuries Suite" Comp. & cond: Eric Coates Orchestra: The New Symphony DECCA LK 4056

151

Film Running Times

FEET	TIME 35mm	TIME 16mm	FEET	TIME 35mm	TIME 16mm	FEET	TIME 35mm	TIME 16mm
1	0.6	1.6	59	37.8	1m 34.4	117	1m 14.9	3m 07.2
2	1.3	3.2	60	38.4	1m 36.0	118	1m 15.5	3m 08.8
3	1.9	4.8	61	39.0	1m 37.6	119	1m 16.2	3m 10.4
4	2.6	6.4	62	39.7	1m 39.2	120	1m 16.8	3m 12.0
5	3.2	8.0	63	40.3	1m 40.8	121	1m 17.4	3m 13.6
6	3.8	9.6	64	41.0	1m 42.4	122	1m 18.1	3m 15.2
7	4.5	11.2	65	41.6	1m 44.0	123	1m 18.7	3m 16.8
8	5.1	12.8	66	42.3	1m 45.6	124	1m 19.4	3m 18.4
9	5.8	14.4	67	42.9	1m 47.2	125	1m 20.0	3m 20.0
10	6.4	16.0	68	43.5	1m 48.8	126	1m 20.7	3m 21.6
11	7.0	17.6	69	44.2	1m 50.4	127	1m 21.3	3m 23.2
12	7.7	19.2	70	44.8	1m 52.0	128	1m 21.9	3m 24.8
13	8.3	20.8	71	45.5	1m 53.6	129	1m 22.6	3m 26.4
14	9.0	22.4	72	46.1	1m 55.2	130	1m 23.2	3m 28.0
15	9.6	24.0	73	46.7	1m 56.8	131	1m 23.8	3m 29.6
16	10.2	25.6	74	47.4	1m 58.4	132	1m 24.5	3m 31.2
17	10.9	27.2	75	48.0	2m 00.0	133	1m 25.1	3m 32.8
18	11.5	28.8	76	48.6	2m 01.0	134	1m 25.8	3m 34.4
19	12.2	30.4	77	49.3	2m 03.2	135	1m 26.4	3m 36.0
20	12.8	32.0	78	49.9	2m 04.8	136	1m 27.0	3m 37.6
21	13.4	33.6	79	50.6	2m 06.4	137	1m 27.7	3m 39.2
22	14.1	35.2	80	51.2	2m 08.0	138	1m 28.3	3m 40.8
23	14.7	36.8	81	51.9	2m 09.6	139	1m 29.0	3m 42.2
24	15.4	38.4	82	52.5	2m 11.2	140	1m 29.6	3m 44.0
25	16.0	40.0	83	53.1	2m 12.8	141	1m 30.2	3m 45.6
26	16.7	41.6	84	53.8	2m 14.4	142	1m 30.9	3m 47.2
27	17.3	43.2	85	54.4	2m 16.0	143	1m 31.5	3m 48.8
28	17.9	44.8	86	55.0	2m 17.6	144	1m 32.2	3m 50.4
29	18.6	46.4	87	55.7	2m 19.2	145	1m 32.8	3m 52.0
30	19.2	48.0	88	56.3	2m 20.8	146	1m 33.4	3m 53.6
31	19.8	49.6	89	57.0	2m 22.4	147	1m 34.1	3m 55.2
32	20.5	51.2	90	57.6	2m 24.0	148	1m 34.7	3m 56.8
33	21.1	52.8	91	58.2	2m 25.6	149	1m 35.4	3m 58.4
34	21.8	54.4	92	58.9	2m 27.2	150	1m 36.0	4m 00.0
35	22.4	56.0	93	59.5	2m 28.8	151	1m 36.6	4m 01.6
36	23.0	57.6	94	1m 00.2	2m 30.4	152	1m 37.3	4m 03.2
37	23.7	59.2	95	1m 00.8	2m 32.0	153	1m 37.9	4m 04.8
38	24.3	1m 00.8	96	1m 01.4	2m 33.6	154	1m 38.6	4m 06.4
39	25.0	1m 02.4	97	1m 02.1	2m 35.2	155	1m 39.2	4m 08.0
40	25.6	1m 04.0	98	1m 02.8	2m 36.8	156	1m 39.8	4m 09.6
41	26.2	1m 05.6	99	1m 03.4	2m 38.4	157	1m 40.5	4m 11.2
42	26.9	1m 07.2	100	1m 04.0	2m 40.0	158	1m 41.1	4m 12.8
43	27.5	1m 08.8	101	1m 04.6	2m 41.6	159	1m 41.8	4m 14.4
44	28.2	1m 10.4	102	1m 05.3	2m 43.2	160	1m 42.4	4m 16.0
45	28.8	1m 12.0	103	1m 05.9	2m 44.8	161	1m 43.0	4m 17.6
46	29.4	1m 13.6	104	1m 06.6	2m 46.4	162	1m 43.7	4m 19.2
47	30.1	1m 15.2	105	1m 07.2	2m 48.0	163	1m 44.3	4m 20.8
48	30.7	1m 16.8	106	1m 07.8	2m 49.6	164	1m 45.0	4m 22.4
49	31.4	1m 18.4	107	1m 08.5	2m 51.2	165	1m 45.6	4m 24.0
50	32.0	1m 20.0	108	1m 09.1	2m 52.8	166	1m 46.3	4m 25.6
51	32.6	1m 21.6	109	1m 09.8	2m 54.4	167	1m 46.9	4m 27.2
52	33.3	1m 23.2	110	1m 10.4	2m 56.0	168	1m 47.5	4m 28.8
53	33.9	1m 24.8	111	1m 11.0	2m 57.6	169	1m 48.2	4m 30.4
54	34.6	1m 26.4	112	1m 11.7	2m 59.2	170	1m 48.8	4m 32.0
55	35.2	1m 28.0	113	1m 12.3	3m 00.8	171	1m 49.5	4m 33.6
56	35.8	1m 29.6	114	1m 13.0	3m 02.4	172	1m 50.1	4m 35.2
57	36.5	1m 32.2	115	1m 13.6	3m 04.0	173	1m 50.7	4m 36.8
58	37.1	1m 32.8	116	1m 14.2	3m 05.6	174	1m 51.4	4m 38.4

FEET	TIME		FEET	TIME		FEET	TIME	
	35mm	16mm		35mm	16mm		35mm	16mm
175	1m 52.0	4m 40.0	236	2m 31.0	6m 17.6	297	3m 10.1	7m 55.2
176	1m 52.6	4m 41.6	237	2m 31.7	6m 19.2	298	3m 10.8	7m 56.8
177	1m 53.3	4m 43.2	238	2m 32.3	6m 20.8	299	3m 11.4	7m 58.4
178	1m 53.9	4m 44.8	239	2m 33.0	6m 22.4	300	3m 12.0	8m 00.0
179	1m 54.6	4m 46.6	240	2m 33.6	6m 24.0	301	3m 12.6	8m 01.6
180	1m 55.2	4m 48.0	241	2m 34.2	6m 25.6	302	3m 13.3	8m 03.2
181	1m 55.9	4m 49.6	242	2m 34.9	6m 27.2	303	3m 13.9	8m 04.8
182	1m 56.5	4m 51.2	243	2m 35.5	6m 28.8	304	3m 14.6	8m 06.4
183	1m 57.1	4m 52.8	244	2m 36.2	6m 30.4	305	3m 15.2	8m 08.0
184	1m 57.8	4m 54.4	245	2m 36.8	6m 32.0	306	3m 15.8	8m 09.6
185	1m 58.4	4m 56.0	246	2m 37.4	6m 33.6	307	3m 16.5	8m 11.2
186	1m 59.0	4m 57.6	247	2m 38.1	6m 35.2	308	3m 17.1	8m 12.8
187	1m 59.7	4m 59.2	248	2m 38.7	6m 36.8	309	3m 17.8	8m 14.4
188	2m 00.3	5m 00.8	249	2m 39.4	6m 38.4	310	3m 18.4	8m 16.0
189	2m 01.0	5m 02.4	250	2m 40.0	6m 40.0	311	3m 19.0	8m 17.6
190	2m 01.6	5m 04.0	251	2m 40.6	6m 41.6	312	3m 19.7	8m 19.2
191	2m 02.2	5m 05.6	252	2m 41.3	6m 43.2	313	3m 20.3	8m 20.8
192	2m 02.9	5m 07.2	253	2m 41.9	6m 44.8	314	3m 21.0	8m 22.4
193	2m 03.5	5m 08.8	254	2m 42.6	6m 46.4	315	3m 21.6	8m 24.0
194	2m 04.2	5m 10.4	255	2m 43.2	6m 48.0	316	3m 22.2	8m 25.6
195	2m 04.8	5m 12.0	256	2m 43.8	6m 49.6	317	3m 22.9	8m 27.2
196	2m 05.4	5m 13.6	257	2m 44.5	6m 51.2	318	3m 23.6	8m 28.8
197	2m 06.1	5m 15.2	258	2m 45.1	6m 52.8	319	3m 24.2	8m 30.4
198	2m 06.8	5m 16.8	259	2m 45.8	6m 54.4	320	3m 24.8	8m 32.0
199	2m 07.4	5m 18.4	260	2m 46.4	6m 56.0	321	3m 25.4	8m 33.6
200	2m 08.0	5m 20.0	261	2m 47.0	6m 57.6	322	3m 26.1	8m 35.2
201	2m 08.6	5m 21.6	262	2m 47.7	6m 59.2	323	3m 26.7	8m 36.8
202	2m 09.3	5m 23.2	263	2m 48.3	7m 00.8	324	3m 27.4	8m 38.4
203	2m 09.9	5m 24.8	264	2m 49.0	7m 02.4	325	3m 28.0	8m 40.0
204	2m 10.6	5m 26.4	265	2m 49.6	7m 04.0	326	3m 28.7	8m 41.6
205	2m 11.2	5m 28.0	266	2m 50.3	7m 05.6	327	3m 29.3	8m 43.2
206	2m 11.8	5m 29.6	267	2m 50.9	7m 07.2	328	3m 29.9	8m 44.8
207	2m 12.5	5m 31.2	268	2m 51.5	7m 08.8	329	3m 30.6	8m 46.4
208	2m 13.1	5m 32.8	269	2m 52.2	7m 10.4	330	3m 31.2	8m 48.0
209	2m 13.8	5m 34.4	270	2m 52.8	7m 12.0	331	3m 31.8	8m 49.6
210	2m 14.4	5m 36.0	271	2m 53.5	7m 13.6	332	3m 32.5	8m 51.2
211	2m 15.0	5m 37.6	272	2m 54.1	7m 15.2	333	3m 33.1	8m 52.8
212	2m 15.7	5m 39.2	273	2m 54.7	7m 16.8	334	3m 33.8	8m 54.4
213	2m 16.3	5m 40.8	274	2m 55.4	7m 18.4	335	3m 34.4	8m 56.0
214	2m 17.0	5m 42.4	275	2m 56.0	7m 20.0	336	3m 35.0	8m 57.6
215	2m 17.6	5m 44.0	276	2m 56.6	7m 21.6	337	3m 35.7	8m 59.2
216	2m 18.2	5m 45.6	277	2m 57.3	7m 23.2	338	3m 36.3	9m 00.8
217	2m 18.9	5m 47.2	278	2m 57.9	7m 24.8	339	3m 37.0	9m 02.4
218	2m 19.6	5m 48.8	279	2m 58.6	7m 26.4	340	3m 37.6	9m 04.0
219	2m 20.2	5m 50.4	280	2m 59.2	7m 28.0	341	3m 38.2	9m 05.6
220	2m 20.8	5m 52.0	281	2m 59.9	7m 29.6	342	3m 38.9	9m 07.2
221	2m 21.4	5m 53.6	282	3m 00.5	7m 31.2	343	3m 39.5	9m 08.8
222	2m 22.1	5m 55.2	283	3m 01.1	7m 32.8	344	3m 40.2	9m 10.4
223	2m 22.7	5m 56.8	284	3m 01.8	7m 34.4	345	3m 40.8	9m 12.0
224	2m 23.4	5m 58.4	285	3m 02.4	7m 36.0	346	3m 41.4	9m 13.6
225	2m 24.0	6m 00.0	286	3m 03.0	7m 37.6	347	3m 42.1	9m 15.2
226	2m 24.7	6m 01.6	287	3m 03.7	7m 39.2	348	3m 42.7	9m 16.8
227	2m 25.3	6m 03.2	288	3m 04.3	7m 40.8	349	3m 43.4	9m 18.4
228	2m 25.9	6m 04.8	289	3m 05.0	7m 42.4	350	3m 44.0	9m 20.0
229	2m 26.6	6m 06.4	290	3m 05.6	7m 44.0	351	3m 44.6	9m 21.6
230	2m 27.2	6m 08.0	291	3m 06.2	7m 45.6	352	3m 45.3	9m 23.2
231	2m 27.8	6m 09.6	292	3m 06.9	7m 47.2	353	3m 45.9	9m 24.8
232	2m 28.5	6m 11.2	293	3m 07.5	7m 48.8	354	3m 46.6	9m 26.4
233	2m 29.1	6m 12.8	294	3m 08.2	7m 50.4	355	3m 47.2	9m 28.0
234	2m 29.8	6m 14.4	295	3m 08.8	7m 52.0	356	3m 47.8	9m 29.6
235	2m 30.4	6m 16.0	296	3m 09.4	7m 53.6	357	3m 48.5	9m 31.2

FEET	TIME		FEET	TIME		FEET	TIME	
	35mm	16mm		35mm	16mm		35mm	16mm
358	3m 49.1	9m 32.8	419	4m 28.2	11m 10.4	480	5m 07.2	12m 48.0
359	3m 49.8	9m 34.4	420	4m 28.8	11m 12.0	481	5m 07.9	12m 49.6
360	3m 50.4	9m 36.0	421	4m 29.4	11m 13.6	482	5m 08.5	12m 51.2
361	3m 51.0	9m 37.6	422	4m 30.1	11m 15.2	483	5m 09.1	12m 52.8
362	3m 51.7	9m 39.2	423	4m 30.7	11m 16.8	484	5m 09.8	12m 54.4
363	3m 52.3	9m 40.8	424	4m 31.4	11m 18.4	485	5m 10.4	12m 56.0
364	3m 53.0	9m 42.4	425	4m 32.0	11m 20.0	486	5m 11.0	12m 57.6
365	3m 53.6	9m 44.0	426	4m 32.7	11m 21.6	487	5m 11.7	12m 59.2
366	3m 54.3	9m 45.6	427	4m 33.3	11m 23.2	488	5m 12.3	13m 00.8
367	3m 54.9	9m 47.2	428	4m 33.9	11m 24.8	489	5m 13.0	13m 02.4
368	3m 55.5	9m 48.8	429	4m 34.6	11m 26.4	490	5m 13.6	13m 04.0
369	3m 56.2	9m 50.4	430	4m 35.2	11m 28.0	491	5m 14.2	13m 05.6
370	3m 56.8	9m 52.0	431	4m 35.8	11m 29.6	492	5m 14.9	13m 07.2
371	3m 57.5	9m 53.6	432	4m 36.5	11m 31.2	493	5m 15.5	13m 08.8
372	3m 58.1	9m 55.2	433	4m 37.1	11m 32.8	494	5m 16.2	13m 10.4
373	3m 58.7	9m 56.8	434	4m 37.8	11m 35.4	495	5m 16.8	13m 12.0
374	3m 59.4	9m 58.4	435	4m 38.4	11m 36.0	496	5m 17.4	13m 13.6
375	4m 00.0	10m 00.0	436	4m 39.0	11m 37.6	497	5m 18.1	13m 15.2
376	4m 00.6	10m 01.6	437	4m 39.7	11m 39.2	498	5m 18.8	13m 16.8
377	4m 01.3	10m 03.2	438	4m 40.3	11m 40.8	499	5m 19.4	13m 18.4
378	4m 01.9	10m 04.8	439	4m 41.0	11m 42.4	500	5m 20.0	13m 20.0
379	4m 02.6	10m 06.4	440	4m 41.6	11m 44.0	501	5m 20.6	13m 21.6
380	4m 03.2	10m 08.0	441	4m 42.2	11m 45.6	502	5m 21.3	13m 23.2
381	4m 03.9	10m 09.6	442	4m 42.9	11m 47.2	503	5m 21.9	13m 24.8
382	4m 04.5	10m 11.2	443	4m 43.5	11m 48.8	504	5m 22.6	13m 26.4
383	4m 05.1	10m 12.8	444	4m 44.2	11m 50.4	505	5m 23.2	13m 28.0
384	4m 05.8	10m 14.4	445	4m 44.8	11m 52.0	506	5m 23.8	13m 29.6
385	4m 06.4	10m 16.0	446	4m 45.4	11m 53.6	507	5m 24.5	13m 31.2
386	4m 07.0	10m 17.6	447	4m 46.1	11m 52.2	508	5m 25.1	13m 32.8
387	4m 07.7	10m 19.2	448	4m 46.7	11m 56.8	509	5m 25.8	13m 34.4
388	4m 08.3	10m 20.8	449	4m 47.4	11m 58.4	510	5m 26.4	13m 36.0
389	4m 09.0	10m 22.4	450	4m 48.0	12m 00.0	511	5m 27.0	13m 37.6
390	4m 09.6	10m 24.0	451	4m 48.6	12m 01.6	512	5m 27.7	13m 39.2
391	4m 10.2	10m 25.6	452	4m 49.3	12m 03.2	513	5m 28.3	13m 40.8
392	4m 10.9	10m 27.2	453	4m 49.9	12m 04.8	514	5m 29.0	13m 42.4
393	4m 11.5	10m 28.8	454	4m 50.6	12m 06.4	515	5m 29.6	13m 44.0
394	4m 12.2	10m 30.4	455	4m 51.2	12m 08.0	516	5m 30.2	13m 45.6
395	4m 12.8	10m 32.0	456	4m 51.8	12m 09.6	517	5m 30.9	13m 47.2
396	4m 13.4	10m 33.6	457	4m 52.5	12m 11.2	518	5m 31.6	13m 48.8
397	4m 14.1	10m 35.2	458	4m 53.1	12m 12.8	519	5m 32.2	13m 50.4
398	4m 14.8	10m 36.8	459	4m 53.8	12m 14.4	520	5m 32.8	13m 52.0
399	4m 15.4	10m 38.4	460	4m 54.4	12m 16.0	521	5m 33.4	13m 53.6
400	4m 16.0	10m 40.0	461	4m 55.0	12m 17.6	522	5m 34.1	13m 55.2
401	4m 16.6	10m 41.6	462	4m 55.7	12m 19.2	523	5m 34.7	13m 56.8
402	4m 17.3	10m 43.2	463	4m 56.3	12m 20.8	524	5m 35.4	13m 58.4
403	4m 17.9	10m 44.8	464	4m 57.0	12m 22.4	525	5m 36.0	14m 00.0
404	4m 18.6	10m 46.4	465	4m 57.6	12m 24.0	526	5m 36.7	14m 01.6
405	4m 19.2	10m 48.0	466	4m 58.3	12m 25.6	527	5m 37.3	14m 03.2
406	4m 19.8	10m 49.6	467	4m 58.9	12m 27.2	528	5m 37.9	14m 04.8
407	4m 20.5	10m 51.2	468	4m 59.5	12m 28.8	529	5m 38.6	14m 06.4
408	4m 21.1	10m 52.8	469	5m 00.2	12m 30.4	530	5m 39.2	14m 08.0
409	4m 21.8	10m 54.4	470	5m 00.8	12m 32.0	531	5m 39.8	14m 09.6
410	4m 22.4	10m 56.0	471	5m 01.5	12m 33.6	532	5m 40.5	14m 11.2
411	4m 23.0	10m 57.6	472	5m 02.1	12m 35.2	533	5m 41.1	14m 12.8
412	4m 23.7	10m 59.2	473	5m 02.7	12m 36.8	534	5m 41.8	14m 14.4
413	4m 24.3	11m 00.8	474	5m 03.4	12m 38.4	535	5m 42.4	14m 16.0
414	4m 25.0	11m 02.4	475	5m 04.0	12m 40.0	536	5m 43.0	14m 17.6
415	4m 25.6	11m 04.0	476	5m 04.6	12m 41.6	537	5m 43.7	14m 19.2
416	4m 26.2	11m 05.6	477	5m 05.3	12m 43.2	538	5m 44.3	14m 20.8
417	4m 26.9	11m 07.2	478	5m 05.9	12m 44.8	539	5m 45.0	14m 22.4
418	4m 27.6	11m 08.8	479	5m 06.6	12m 46.4	540	5m 45.6	14m 24.0

FEET	TIME		FEET	TIME		FEET	TIME	
	35mm	16mm		35mm	16mm		35mm	16mm
541	5m 46.2	14m 25.6	602	6m 25.3	16m 03.2	663	7m 04.3	17m 40.8
542	5m 46.9	14m 27.2	603	6m 25.9	16m 04.8	664	7m 05.0	17m 42.4
543	5m 47.5	14m 28.8	604	6m 26.6	16m 06.4	665	7m 05.6	17m 44.0
544	5m 48.2	14m 30.4	605	6m 27.2	16m 08.0	666	7m 06.3	17m 45.6
545	5m 48.8	14m 32.0	606	6m 27.8	16m 09.6	667	7m 06.9	17m 47.2
546	5m 49.4	14m 33.6	607	6m 28.5	16m 11.2	668	7m 07.5	17m 48.8
547	5m 50.1	14m 35.2	608	6m 29.1	16m 12.8	669	7m 08.2	17m 50.4
548	5m 50.7	14m 36.8	609	6m 29.8	16m 14.4	670	7m 08.8	17m 52.0
549	5m 51.4	14m 38.4	610	6m 30.4	16m 16.0	671	7m 09.5	17m 53.6
550	5m 52.0	14m 40.0	611	6m 31.0	16m 17.6	672	7m 10.1	17m 55.2
551	5m 52.6	14m 41.6	612	6m 31.7	16m 19.2	673	7m 10.7	17m 56.8
552	5m 53.3	14m 43.2	613	6m 32.3	16m 20.8	674	7m 11.4	17m 58.4
553	5m 53.9	14m 44.8	614	6m 33.0	16m 22.4	675	7m 12.0	18m 00.0
554	5m 54.6	14m 46.4	615	6m 33.6	16m 24.0	676	7m 12.6	18m 01.6
555	5m 55.2	14m 48.0	616	6m 34.2	16m 25.6	677	7m 13.3	18m 03.2
556	5m 55.8	14m 49.6	617	6m 34.9	16m 27.2	678	7m 13.9	18m 04.8
557	5m 56.5	14m 51.2	618	6m 35.6	16m 28.8	679	7m 14.6	18m 06.4
558	5m 57.1	14m 52.8	619	6m 36.2	16m 30.4	680	7m 15.2	18m 08.0
559	5m 57.8	14m 54.4	620	6m 36.8	16m 32.0	681	7m 15.9	18m 09.6
560	5m 58.4	14m 56.0	621	6m 37.4	16m 33.6	682	7m 16.5	18m 11.2
561	5m 59.0	14m 57.6	622	6m 38.1	16m 35.2	683	7m 17.1	18m 12.8
562	5m 59.7	14m 59.2	623	6m 38.7	16m 36.8	684	7m 17.8	18m 14.4
563	6m 00.3	15m 00.8	624	6m 39.4	16m 38.4	685	7m 18.4	18m 16.0
564	6m 01.0	15m 02.4	625	6m 40.0	16m 40.0	686	7m 19.0	18m 17.6
565	6m 01.6	15m 04.0	626	6m 40.7	16m 41.6	687	7m 19.7	18m 19.2
566	6m 02.3	15m 05.6	627	6m 41.3	16m 43.2	688	7m 20.3	18m 20.8
567	6m 02.9	15m 07.2	628	6m 41.9	16m 44.8	689	7m 21.0	18m 22.4
568	6m 03.5	15m 08.8	629	6m 42.6	16m 46.4	690	7m 21.6	18m 24.0
569	6m 04.2	15m 10.4	630	6m 43.3	16m 48.0	691	7m 22.2	18m 25.6
570	6m 04.8	15m 12.0	631	6m 43.8	16m 49.6	692	7m 22.9	18m 27.2
571	6m 05.5	15m 13.6	632	6m 44.5	16m 52.2	693	7m 23.5	18m 28.8
572	6m 06.1	15m 15.2	633	6m 45.1	16m 53.8	694	7m 24.2	18m 30.4
573	6m 06.7	15m 16.8	634	6m 45.8	16m 55.4	695	7m 24.8	18m 32.0
574	6m 07.4	15m 18.4	635	6m 46.4	16m 57.6	696	7m 25.4	18m 33.6
575	6m 08.0	15m 20.0	636	6m 47.0	16m 57.6	697	7m 26.1	18m 35.2
576	6m 08.6	15m 21.6	637	6m 47.7	16m 59.2	698	7m 26.8	18m 36.8
577	6m 09.3	15m 23.2	638	6m 48.3	17m 00.8	699	7m 27.4	18m 38.4
578	6m 09.9	15m 24.8	639	6m 49.0	17m 02.4	700	7m 28.0	18m 40.0
579	6m 10.6	15m 26.4	640	6m 49.6	17m 04.0	701	7m 28.6	18m 41.6
580	6m 11.2	15m 28.0	641	6m 50.2	17m 05.6	702	7m 29.3	18m 43.2
581	6m 11.9	15m 29.6	642	6m 50.9	17m 07.2	703	7m 29.9	18m 44.8
582	6m 12.5	15m 31.2	643	6m 51.5	17m 08.8	704	7m 30.6	18m 46.4
583	6m 13.1	15m 32.8	644	6m 52.2	17m 10.4	705	7m 31.2	18m 48.0
584	6m 13.8	15m 34.4	645	6m 52.8	17m 12.0	706	7m 31.8	18m 49.6
585	6m 14.4	15m 36.0	646	6m 53.4	17m 13.6	707	7m 32.5	18m 51.2
586	6m 15.0	15m 37.6	647	6m 54.1	17m 15.2	708	7m 33.1	18m 52.8
587	6m 15.7	15m 39.2	648	6m 54.7	17m 16.8	709	7m 33.8	18m 54.4
588	6m 16.3	15m 40.8	649	6m 55.4	17m 18.4	710	7m 34.4	18m 56.0
589	6m 17.0	15m 42.4	650	6m 56.0	17m 20.0	711	7m 35.0	18m 57.6
590	6m 17.6	15m 44.0	651	6m 56.6	17m 21.6	712	7m 35.7	18m 59.2
591	6m 18.2	15m 45.6	652	6m 57.3	17m 23.2	713	7m 36.6	19m 00.8
592	6m 18.9	15m 47.2	653	6m 57.9	17m 24.8	714	7m 37.0	19m 02.4
593	6m 19.5	15m 48.8	654	6m 58.6	17m 26.4	715	7m 37.6	19m 04.0
594	6m 20.2	15m 50.4	655	6m 59.2	17m 28.0	716	7m 38.2	19m 05.6
595	6m 20.8	15m 52.0	656	6m 59.8	17m 29.6	717	7m 38.9	19m 07.2
596	6m 21.4	15m 53.6	657	7m 00.5	17m 31.2	718	7m 39.6	19m 08.8
597	6m 22.1	15m 55.2	658	7m 01.1	17m 32.8	719	7m 40.2	19m 10.4
598	6m 22.8	15m 56.8	659	7m 01.8	17m 34.4	720	7m 40.8	19m 12.0
599	6m 23.4	15m 58.4	660	7m 02.4	17m 36.0	721	7m 41.4	19m 13.6
600	6m 24.0	16m 00.0	661	7m 03.0	17m 37.6	722	7m 42.1	19m 15.2
601	6m 24.6	16m 01.6	662	7m 03.7	17m 39.2	723	7m 42.7	19m 16.8

FEET	TIME		FEET	TIME		FEET	TIME	
	35mm	16mm		35mm	16mm		35mm	16mm
724	7m 43.4	19m 18.4	785	8m 22.4	20m 56.0	846	9m 01.4	22m 33.6
725	7m 44.0	19m 20.0	786	8m 23.0	20m 57.6	847	9m 02.1	22m 35.2
726	7m 44.7	19m 21.6	787	8m 23.7	20m 59.2	848	9m 02.7	22m 36.8
727	7m 45.3	19m 23.2	788	8m 24.3	21m 00.8	849	9m 03.4	22m 38.4
728	7m 45.9	19m 24.8	789	8m 25.0	21m 02.4	850	9m 04.0	22m 40.0
729	7m 46.6	19m 26.4	790	8m 25.6	21m 04.0	851	9m 04.6	22m 41.6
730	7m 47.2	19m 28.0	791	8m 26.2	21m 05.6	852	9m 05.3	22m 43.2
731	7m 47.8	19m 29.6	792	8m 26.9	21m 07.2	853	9m 05.9	22m 44.8
732	7m 48.5	19m 31.2	793	8m 27.5	21m 08.8	854	9m 06.6	22m 46.4
733	7m 49.1	19m 32.8	794	8m 28.2	21m 10.4	855	9m 07.2	22m 48.0
734	7m 49.8	19m 34.4	795	8m 28.8	21m 12.0	856	9m 07.8	22m 49.6
735	7m 50.4	19m 36.0	796	8m 29.4	21m 13.6	857	9m 08.5	22m 51.2
736	7m 51.0	19m 37.6	797	8m 30.1	21m 15.2	858	9m 09.1	22m 52.8
737	7m 51.7	19m 39.2	798	8m 30.8	21m 16.8	859	9m 09.8	22m 54.4
738	7m 52.3	19m 40.8	799	8m 31.4	21m 18.4	860	9m 10.4	22m 56.0
739	7m 53.0	19m 42.4	800	8m 32.0	21m 20.0	861	9m 11.0	22m 57.6
740	7m 53.6	19m 44.0	801	8m 32.6	21m 21.6	862	9m 11.7	22m 59.2
741	7m 54.2	19m 45.6	802	8m 33.3	21m 23.2	863	9m 12.3	23m 00.8
742	7m 54.9	19m 47.2	803	8m 33.9	21m 24.8	864	9m 13.0	23m 02.4
743	7m 55.5	19m 48.8	804	8m 34.6	21m 26.4	865	9m 13.6	23m 04.0
744	7m 56.2	19m 50.4	805	8m 35.2	21m 28.0	866	9m 14.3	23m 05.6
745	7m 56.8	19m 52.0	806	8m 35.8	21m 29.6	867	9m 14.9	23m 07.2
746	7m 57.4	19m 53.6	807	8m 36.5	21m 31.2	868	9m 15.5	23m 08.8
747	7m 58.1	19m 55.2	808	8m 37.1	21m 32.8	869	9m 16.2	23m 10.4
748	7m 58.7	19m 56.8	809	8m 37.8	21m 34.4	870	9m 16.9	23m 12.0
749	7m 59.4	19m 58.4	810	8m 38.4	21m 36.0	871	9m 17.5	23m 13.6
750	8m 00.0	20m 00.0	811	8m 39.0	21m 37.6	872	9m 18.1	23m 15.2
751	8m 00.6	20m 01.6	812	8m 39.7	21m 39.2	873	9m 18.7	23m 16.8
752	8m 01.3	20m 03.2	813	8m 40.3	21m 40.8	874	9m 19.4	23m 18.4
753	8m 01.9	20m 04.8	814	8m 41.0	21m 42.4	875	9m 20.0	23m 20.0
754	8m 02.6	20m 06.4	815	8m 41.6	21m 44.0	876	9m 20.6	23m 21.6
755	8m 03.2	20m 08.0	816	8m 42.2	21m 45.6	877	9m 21.3	23m 23.2
756	8m 03.8	20m 09.6	817	8m 42.9	21m 47.2	878	9m 21.9	23m 24.8
757	8m 04.5	20m 11.2	818	8m 43.6	21m 48.8	879	9m 22.6	23m 26.4
758	8m 05.1	20m 12.8	819	8m 44.2	21m 50.4	880	9m 23.2	23m 28.0
759	8m 05.8	20m 14.4	820	8m 44.8	21m 52.0	881	9m 23.9	23m 29.6
760	8m 06.4	20m 16.0	821	8m 45.4	21m 53.6	882	9m 24.5	23m 31.2
761	8m 07.0	20m 17.6	822	8m 46.1	21m 55.2	883	9m 25.1	23m 32.8
762	8m 07.7	20m 19.2	823	8m 46.7	21m 56.8	884	9m 25.8	23m 34.4
763	8m 08.3	20m 20.8	824	8m 47.4	21m 58.4	885	9m 26.4	23m 36.0
764	8m 09.0	20m 22.4	825	8m 48.0	22m 00.0	886	9m 27.0	23m 37.6
765	8m 09.6	20m 24.0	826	8m 48.7	22m 01.6	887	9m 27.7	23m 39.2
766	8m 10.3	24m 25.6	827	8m 49.3	22m 03.2	888	9m 28.3	23m 40.8
767	8m 10.9	20m 27.2	828	8m 49.9	22m 04.8	889	9m 29.0	23m 42.4
768	8m 11.5	20m 28.8	829	8m 50.6	22m 06.4	890	9m 29.6	23m 44.0
769	8m 12.2	20m 30.4	830	8m 51.2	22m 08.0	891	9m 30.2	23m 45.6
770	8m 12.8	20m 32.0	831	8m 51.8	22m 09.6	892	9m 30.9	23m 47.2
771	8m 13.5	20m 33.6	832	8m 52.5	22m 11.2	893	9m 31.5	23m 48.8
772	8m 14.1	20m 35.2	833	8m 53.1	22m 12.8	894	9m 32.2	23m 50.4
773	8m 14.7	20m 36.8	834	8m 53.8	22m 14.4	895	9m 32.8	23m 52.0
774	8m 15.4	20m 38.4	835	8m 54.4	22m 16.0	896	9m 33.4	23m 53.6
775	8m 16.0	20m 40.0	836	8m 55.0	22m 17.6	897	9m 34.1	23m 55.2
776	8m 16.7	20m 41.6	837	8m 55.7	22m 19.2	898	9m 34.8	23m 56.8
777	8m 17.3	20m 43.2	838	8m 56.3	22m 20.8	899	9m 35.4	23m 58.4
778	8m 17.9	20m 44.8	839	8m 57.0	22m 22.4	900	9m 36.0	24m 00.0
779	8m 18.6	20m 46.4	840	8m 57.6	22m 24.0	901	9m 36.6	24m 01.6
780	8m 19.2	20m 48.0	841	8m 58.2	22m 25.6	902	9m 37.3	24m 03.2
781	8m 19.9	20m 49.6	842	8m 58.9	22m 27.2	903	9m 37.9	24m 04.8
782	8m 20.5	20m 51.2	843	8m 59.5	22m 28.8	904	9m 38.6	24m 06.4
783	8m 21.1	20m 52.8	844	9m 00.2	22m 30.4	905	9m 39.2	24m 08.0
784	8m 21.8	20m 54.4	845	9m 00.8	22m 32.0	906	9m 39.8	24m 09.6

FEET	TIME		FEET	TIME		FEET	TIME	
	35mm	16mm		35mm	16mm		35mm	16mm
907	9m 40.5	24m 11.2	939	10m 01.0	25m 02.4	971	10m 21.5	25m 53.6
908	9m 41.1	24m 12.8	940	10m 01.6	25m 04.0	972	10m 22.1	25m 55.2
909	9m 41.8	24m 14.4	941	10m 02.2	25m 05.6	973	10m 22.7	25m 56.8
910	9m 42.4	24m 16.0	942	10m 02.9	25m 07.2	974	10m 23.4	25m 58.4
911	9m 43.0	24m 17.6	943	10m 03.5	25m 08.8	975	10m 24.0	26m 00.0
912	9m 43.7	24m 19.2	944	10m 04.2	25m 10.4	976	10m 24.6	26m 01.6
913	9m 44.3	24m 20.8	945	10m 04.8	25m 12.0	977	10m 25.3	26m 03.2
914	9m 45.0	24m 22.4	946	10m 05.4	25m 13.6	978	10m 25.9	26m 04.8
915	9m 45.6	24m 24.0	947	10m 06.1	25m 15.2	979	10m 26.6	26m 06.4
916	9m 46.2	24m 25.6	948	10m 06.7	25m 16.8	980	10m 27.2	26m 08.0
917	9m 46.9	24m 27.2	949	10m 07.4	25m 18.4	981	10m 27.9	26m 09.6
918	9m 47.6	24m 28.8	950	10m 08.0	25m 20.0	982	10m 28.5	26m 11.2
919	9m 48.2	24m 30.4	951	10m 08.6	25m 21.6	983	10m 29.1	26m 12.8
920	9m 48.8	24m 32.0	952	10m 09.3	25m 23.3	984	10m 29.8	26m 14.4
921	9m 49.4	24m 33.6	953	10m 09.9	25m 24.8	985	10m 30.4	26m 16.0
922	9m 50.1	24m 35.2	954	10m 10.6	25m 26.4	986	10m 31.0	26m 17.6
923	9m 50.7	24m 36.8	955	10m 11.2	25m 28.0	987	10m 31.7	26m 19.2
924	9m 51.4	24m 38.4	956	10m 11.8	25m 29.6	988	10m 32.3	26m 20.8
925	9m 52.0	24m 40.0	957	10m 12.5	25m 31.2	989	10m 33.0	26m 22.4
926	9m 52.7	24m 41.6	958	10m 13.1	25m 32.8	990	10m 33.6	26m 24.0
927	9m 53.3	24m 43.2	959	10m 13.8	25m 34.4	991	10m 34.2	26m 25.6
928	9m 53.9	24m 44.8	960	10m 14.4	25m 36.0	992	10m 34.9	26m 27.2
929	9m 54.6	24m 46.4	961	10m 15.0	25m 37.6	993	10m 35.5	26m 28.8
930	9m 55.2	24m 48.0	962	10m 15.7	25m 39.2	994	10m 36.2	26m 30.4
931	9m 55.8	24m 49.6	963	10m 16.3	25m 40.8	995	10m 36.8	26m 32.0
932	9m 56.5	24m 51.2	964	10m 17.0	25m 42.4	996	10m 37.4	26m 33.6
933	9m 57.1	24m 52.8	965	10m 17.6	25m 44.0	997	10m 38.1	26m 35.2
934	9m 57.8	24m 54.4	966	10m 18.3	25m 45.6	998	10m 38.8	26m 36.8
935	9m 58.4	24m 56.0	967	10m 18.9	25m 47.2	999	10m 39.4	26m 38.4
936	9m 59.0	24m 57.6	968	10m 19.5	25m 48.8	1000	10m 40.0	26m 40.0
937	9m 59.7	24m 59.2	969	10m 20.2	25m 50.4			
938	10m 00.3	25m 00.8	970	10m 20.9	25m 52.0			

Glossary

Academy (134) American Academy of Motion Picture Arts and Sciences. The Academy frame is the 'standard' shaped aperture (as opposed to Widescreen, Cinemascope etc.)

Action (52, 80) 1. Command used by director to start the action (below). 2. What the actor or actors actually do during the shot. 3. Used to describe the visual component of a shot as opposed to the sound.

Angle (18, 24, 28) The various shots of the same subject matter, taken from different positions are often referred to as angles.

Art Director (114) Person responsible for designing the *set* on which the film is being shot. Often known in television as *Designer*.

Boom Means of suspension for the microphone. Can range from a complicated contraption on wheels with a platform for the operator to stand on, to an extendable pole which he holds in his hands.

'Camera Left' Direction of position or movement of anything taking place in front of the camera as viewed from behind the camera. A man facing the camera moves 'camera left' if he walks to *his* right. Opposite movement is 'camera right'.

Cameraman Person responsible for photographing the production. On a major production, may be known as Director of Photography or Lighting Cameraman. He does not necessarily operate the camera.

Camera Operator (26) Person who operates the film camera. On smaller productions this can either be the cameraman or his assistant.

Camera Report Document made out by the assistant cameraman to advise the processing laboratory and the film editor, which describes and catalogues the exposed film.

Camera Roll Each roll of unexposed film stock placed in the camera is given a number.

Clapperboard Small blackboard with a hinged arm at the top. At the beginning of each shot an assistant cameraman chalks the slate and take number on the board, announces them verbally for the benefit of the sound recordist and snaps the arm down with a bang. The exact point of impact is used by the film editor's assistant when synchronising picture and sound.

Clapperboy The most junior member of the camera department on a large production loads the film into the magazine and is responsible for marking each shot.

Close Shot (28) Shot highlighting a specific action, person, thing.

Complementary two-shot (30) If a conversation between two people is covered by two-shots, each favouring one character, the two-shots are said to be complementary.

Continuity Notes (74) Documents completed by the continuity girl for each shot taken. In addition to notes on continuity, information on length and acceptability of each take is included.

Cut (80) 1. Command given by the director during or at the end of a take to stop it all happening. 2. Point of transition between two shots as determined by the film editor.

Cutaways (26, 32) 1. Shots of specific parts of the scene. 2. Shots used to highlight particular pieces of action. 3. Shots used by the editor to avoid a jump cut.

158

Designer See *Art Director*.

Director (26) Person who directs the action, camera crew etc. in the making of a film.

Dressing Material used to enhance the set (qv) (furniture, pictures, leaves, cobwebs, animals, extras (qv) etc.).

Dressers A costume assistant who assists artists with their costumes.

Exposure Meter Device used by the cameraman to determine the level of illumination of the scene, and thus the aperture setting, or 'f' stop, to be set on the camera lens.

Film Editor (20, 84) Person responsible for cutting the individual shots of the film together after shooting.

Film Gauges At one time or another the following widths of motion picture film have been used; 70mm, 65mm, 35mm, 17.5mm, 16mm, Super 16mm, 9.5mm, 8mm, Super 8mm. Except for some very large-scale productions using the two largest gauges and a few low-budget feature films shot on Super 16mm, proessional film making uses 35mm or 16mm.

Film Unit (18) Collective term for everyone involved in the making of a film.

First Assistant On a feature film, there will be several assistant directors. The first assistant is the most senior. In television productions the first assistant is often called the PA (Production Assistant) and the second assistant the AFM (Assistant Floor Manager).

Focal Length (26) The field of view of a lens is determined by its focal length. The longer the focal length, the narrower the field. A 'zoom' lens is one with *variable* focal length, and a 'zoom in' is effected by increasing the focal length.

Footage Counter (142) Device fitted to cameras, editing equipment and dubbing theatres giving a digital indication of the amount of film run through.

Frame (142) 1. Each individual photograph on a strip of cinè film. A film camera runs at 24 or 25 frames per second. 2. The term can be used to refer to the area the camera is looking at, hence 'leaving frame'. 3. To compose a shot, the cameraman is told to 'frame up' on the door, hence 'framing'.

Gaffer Slang term for chief or head.

Job or Production Number Every production is given a number which is used mainly in costing.

Jump Cut An editing point in a finished film where a piece of the action has obviously been left out.

Location (78) Place where any film or part of a film is shot other than a studio.

'Mark it' Command normally given by the cameraman for the clapperboy (qv) to identify the take.

Master Shot (26) Often the wide angle. Shot containing all the action into which cutaways are inserted.

Master Sound Track Length of magnetic film recorded in the dubbing theatre which contains all the components of the film's sound. Often known as 'the final mix' it is always copied to ensure against accidents.

Polaroid (74) Trade name of a still camera which is capable of processing the photograph you've just taken in less than a minute.

Processing (124) The development, printing etc. of the film which takes place at the laboratory.

Production Manager Person responsible for the budget, administration, transport, accommodation etc. In television, the PA usually also acts as the production manager.

Re-light (16) Each time the lights are moved for a different shot.

Rushes (126) Technically the 'rushed first prints' of yesterday's shooting. Usually the term refers to the picture and sound before ending, either before or after processing and transfer. After synchronisation of picture and sound, we have 'sync rushes'.

Schedule (122) Document cataloguing the administrative arrangements for the shooting of each scene.

Second Assistant See *First Assistant*.

Set Essentially the scenery in front of which the action is taking place. In practice the precise area where the shooting is going on.

Set-up Each time the camera is moved requiring a re-light (qv).

Shot (24, 140) In shooting, a length of film taken without stopping the camera. In editing, a length of film between two cuts.

Shot List (24) A list of shots in the order of shooting compiled at the time of filming; or: (136) A list of shots as they appear in the editied film after editing.

Single (26) Shot of one actor in a multiple character situation as opposed to a two-shot, three-shot etc.

Slate Number (76) Number given to each shot in shooting. the shot itself is often called a slate.

Sound Recordist Person in charge of the sound in shooting.

Sync (Sound) (78) A sync shot has interlocked sound taken at the same time, as opposed to a mute shot where no sound is recorded, or: (122) (Verb) abbrev. of the operation of synchronising rushes.

Sound Roll Number Number given to each roll of tape or magnetic film placed on the recording machine.

Sparks slang term for electrician.

'Speed' Confirmation given by sound recordist that the recorder is running and has 'come up to speed'.

Spotlight Standard British reference manual of actors.

Third Assistant See *First Assistant*. In television, the floor assistant is the equivalent of the third assistant.

'Turn over' Command given to camera operator to switch on camera.

Wildtrack (126) Sound recording made without the recorder interlocked to a camera.

Zoom Handle (26) Lever on zoom lens which adjusts focal length.

Zoom Lens (26) Lens of which the focal length can be varied. By increasing the focal length the subject appears nearer the camera. If the focal length is increased or decreased while the camera is running the result shot includes a zoom in or a zoom out.

160